The Making of Living Stones

A Bible Study on Ephesians:
Leader's Notes

Eunice Kwok

The Making of Living Stones:
A Bible Study on Ephesians (Leader's Notes)

Copyright © 2024 Eunice Kwok

Eunice Kwok has asserted her right under the Copyright, Designs and Patents Act 1988 to be identified as the Author of this work.

All rights reserved. No portion of this work may be reproduced, stored in a retrieval system, or transmitted in any form or by any means – electronic, mechanical, photocopy, recording, or any other – except for brief quotation in printed review, without the prior permission of the copyright owner.

All scripture quotations in this work are taken from the Holy Bible, English Standard Version, published by HarperCollins*Publishers*, © 2001 Crossway Bibles, a publishing ministry of Good New Publishers. Used by permission. All rights reserved.

ISBN: 9798333821805

Cover design by Eunice Kwok

DEDICATED TO

Edwin,
with whom I learn about
'the profound mystery' of marriage
which refers to Christ and the church

Adeline and Albert
to whom I am the mother,
an imitator of God to bring them up
in the discipline and instruction of the Lord
as commanded

(Ephesians 5:1-2, 22-6:4)

So then you are no longer strangers and aliens, but you are fellow citizens with the saints and members of the household of God, built on the foundation of the apostles and prophets, Christ Jesus himself being the cornerstone, in whom the whole structure, being joined together, grows into a holy temple in the Lord. In him you also are being built together into a dwelling place for God by the Spirit.

(Ephesians 2:19-22)

Contents

PREFACE vii
1. An Overview [1:1-2] 1
2. A Cascade of Blessings [1:3-14] 10
3. Lack no Good Thing [1:15-23] 24
4. Zombies Come Alive [2:1-10] 37
5. Divided No More [2:11-22] 52
6. Without Limits [3:1-21] 66
7. Becoming Worthy [4:1-16] 82
8. Radically New [4:17-24] 100
9. Newness of life [4:25-32] 109
10. A New Gait: Love and Light [5:1-14] 120
11. A New Gait: Wisdom [5:15-21] 133
12. Husbands and Wives [5:22-33] 143
13. Children and Slaves [6:1-9] 155
14. Spiritual Warfare [6:10-24] 168

PREFACE

Something that has etched on your memory you will never forget. It was June 1997; Gareth Griffiths (27) from the UK was holidaying in Florida. No stranger to adventure sports, he attempted tandem skydiving. The sport involves the novice being strapped to an instructor, and the pair free fall for the first part of the descent, normally about 30 seconds, before the parachute is released for them to glide to earth. On that fateful day, a routine jump turned into tragedy when both the main and reserve parachutes failed to open. The pair was 5000ft above ground, falling at 120 miles per hour. The instructor, Michael Costello (42), was an experienced parachutist. He twisted around in his harness and wrapped himself around his student to cushion him from the blow of landing. His wife said that it was very intentional of him. In a split-second decision, the instructor made the ultimate sacrifice to save his student. He died on impact while his student did, miraculously, live.[1]

Watching the incident being reported on the news, I

---

[1] https://www.heraldscotland.com/news/12317449.skydiver-makes-ultimate-sacrifice-instructor-dies-saving-his-student/;
https://www.independent.co.uk/news/the-man-who-fell-to-earth-and-lived-to-tell-the-tale-1257796.html

remember thinking, 'One person died in order that the other could live; how would the student live from now on? Would he feel that he owes his life to this instructor and his life is not his own anymore? Would he feel obliged to live a life worthy of his instructor's ultimate sacrifice? Surely, he would not live in such a way that would dishonour his instructor. This would require him to get to know who his instructor was as a person ....' Immediately I saw the striking parallels between this chain of thoughts and the call of Christian lives. Two things came crystal clear to my mind: (1) the expectation of Christ's followers to live for Christ in response to His sacrifice for them is justified even with our own reason; and (2) while no one would fail to see the action of the instructor as heroic that inspires praise and respect, Christ's sacrifice for us, the underserving sinners, is often scorned! It shows our depravity and that we can only be saved by grace through faith just as Paul has taught us in Ephesians (2:1-10).

It so happened that this year (2024) was an occasion that called us to remember those to whom we all were indebted. To mark the 80th anniversary of D-Day, 1475 silhouettes by 'Standing with Giants' were sent to British Normandy Memorial for display between 21 April and 31 August, representing the number of fatalities under British command on 6 June 1944. 'For Your Tomorrow, We Gave Our Today.' Standing with the life-sized silhouettes makes a poignant scene and reminds us that freedom is not free and we live in the shadow of their sacrifice. Among them, many were only teenagers. They might not be known to us personally but they all had loved ones who mourned their deaths. Freedom is costly and the pain of loss is only allayed when the cause they died for is worthy. We are whom they died for; do we live a life worthy of their sacrifice? 'Lest we forget', a phrase commonly used in war memorial services and commemorative occasions, is a plea for remembrance of past sacrifices. That the plea is necessary reflects our forgetfulness. When we lose the context of our existence and our identity is in crisis, we get confused and insecure. God knows our weakness; this is why He commands us to *remember* repeatedly. *Only take care, and keep our soul diligently, lest you forget the things that your eyes have seen and lest they depart from your heart all the days of your life* (Deut. 4:9a). Remember, lest we forget who we are.

The letter to the Ephesians calls us to remember too: remember who we once were and are no longer; remember who we are now, a new creation in union with Christ, lest we forget and revert to live in our former way of life. We often think, and this is where we often err, that our salvation is about us, the individuals, and our passage to heaven. This of course is true but not all. Paul's letter to the Ephesians is clear that the ultimate purpose of the gospel is the new humanity created under the headship of Christ in unity, *to the praise of his glory* (1:12). This is the gospel of peace, which not only restores us to God but also broke down the long established and seemingly impregnable dividing wall between Jews and Gentiles, and *reconcile(s) us both to God in one body through the cross, thereby killing the hostility* (2:16). Furthermore, God's cosmic plan is *for the fullness of time, to unite all things in him, things in heaven and things on earth* (1:10). So, God's salvation plan for us is to save us individually in order that we are united as one people of Christ and display *the manifold wisdom of God* (see Session 6 Q6 and Q10). This is glorious because division has been plaguing human society for as long as history can remember, and human attempts on unity are never long lasting. The fallout is that broken marriages and broken homes are commonplace in our everyday life while wars and conflicts are recurring in human history.

Our calling is not to be churchless Christians even though this has recently become popular in our highly individualistic society. Churchless Christians are those who see faith as personal and pursue spirituality in some sort of fluid 'church' which demands no commitment by, for example, listening to sermon online, meeting a 'community' of like-minded people on social media and fellowshipping with their small groups at a café in a format of mutual discipleship with no established authority structure. DeYoung and Kluck (2009)[2] coins the trend 'decorpulation', as increasingly people are looking for a Christianity that cuts off the body (i.e. the institutional church). It is not difficult to understand why this can be attractive. Church is hard because the ideal is high. The reality can be disappointing because it is a body of sinners and relationships can be trying. In Ephesians, we see that church is a mystical entity and cannot be understood by human wisdom. What bonds the members together in oneness and what gives it its life and dynamics is out of this world, literally. We cannot analyse it using a management model, for example. If we judge it by what is visible and do not love it enough to function as full members, we are bound to be disillusioned because more likely than not, it does not live up to our expectations. Relationships in our personal life are consuming and absorbing enough as they are; who needs extra hassles from relationships we can do away with? Quitting church or never joining one then looks highly attractive. When we are tempted by this thought, *remember* that Christ declares 'I will build my church' (Matt. 16:18) and that He died to purchase His bride. His purpose is to knit her into a sophisticated body of diverse gifts, to be an instrument for His use and glory. We dare not insult His church, no matter how imperfect she is on this side of heaven. Obedience to God's will is to persevere with church, and when we do, we grow and mature *together* as followers of Christ, receiving the abundant blessing He has intended for us through our church membership. This *togetherness* is a key characteristic of the church explored in Ephesians.

Church as a collective body is made up of redeemed individuals. Having given us a vision of the church as a unit,

---

[2] DeYoung, Kevin & Kluck, Ted (2009) *Why We Love the Church: in praise of institutions and organised religion*, Moody Publishers.

Preface

Paul moves on to instruct its members in their new way of life, urging them to lead a life *worthy of the calling to which (they) have been called* (4:1). This *newness* that has come to believers was unknown in the first century. Paul therefore painstakingly spells out for the Gentile believers this revolutionary lifestyle that would in turn support the collective life of the church. Apostle Peter calls the individual members of the church *living stones, built up as a spiritual house* (1 Pet. 2:4-5). The beauty in this picture is that the *unity* of the church is not achieved by *uniformity* but by *plurality*; these *living stones* are each unique in shape and size with their *varied grace* (4:7) but fitted perfectly with one another to form a united whole in the Potter's hand which fashions each of them in this life where the quarry is (see Session 5 Q8 and Session 7). Rather than being like a brick wall of modern time with uniform bricks, God's masterpiece is more like a polygonal wall of ancient time, which was built from stones of irregular shapes and sizes without mortar or cement. The cover of this publication shows the one in Delphi, Greece, built in 548 BC. It has withstood the test of time and numerous earthquakes for the past 2500 years!

Now come with me as I make this further point with this vision of the church before us. In an age of lost identity and anxiety, it is ground-breaking to know that our identity, our greatness, or the meaning of our existence is found not in ourselves or our talents but in God's placement of us in His cosmic plan! That meaning lasts the eternity! For the redeemed, our value is founded in our union with Christ and expressed in our unique placement in His Church as living stones. There we are made whole. The question, as Jesus asked the invalid by the Bethesda pool in John 5:6, is, 'Would you like to be made whole?' You may think, of course, an invalid would like to be healed, but would Jesus ask a redundant question? How many have rejected Christ? Even among Christ's followers, how many try to avoid the chisel in the making of living stones and being fitted into His church? Would you submit willingly to God's pruning? *Be filled with the Spirit* (5:18), Paul exhorts us. Yes, it is an action done to us but we have to cooperate in our submission to His work in us. And that lifestyle requires discipline and diligence. 'Would you like to be made whole?' turns out to be the most soul-searching question raised by studying Ephesians.

In terms of structure, Ephesians is clearly a letter of two halves, demonstrating explicitly the grammar of Christian faith (see Session 1 Q9). The basic rule of the gospel grammar is that *divine imperatives* are logically preceded by and grounded in *divine indicatives*. That is, divine imperatives are nothing but descriptions of our inexorable response to be lived out in our lives to divine indicatives of who God is and what He has done. This may not be the actual order appeared in any given passage but it is in Ephesians, with the first three chapters on divine indicatives and the last three on divine imperatives. We must resist the temptation to take the second half out of context and attempt holy living ourselves, not least because this will be futile effort. To understand Paul's instructions, we must remember that the second half flows out from the first half which propels our Christian living; our *new* lifestyle is built on and fuelled by our knowledge of God. The recap for each chapter purposefully makes this point explicit to the reader.

The references consulted for this study are as follows:
- John MacArthur (1986) *The MacArthur New Testament Commentary on Ephesians*, Moody Publishers;
- Calvin's commentary on the letter to the Ephesians, available online;
- Sinclair B Ferguson (2005) *Let's Study Ephesians*, The Banner of Truth Trust;
- *Reformation Study Bible* (2015), Reformation Trust Publishing;
- David Jackman (2012) *He is Our Peace: Ephesians*, Pathway Bible Guides, Matthias Media.

The preparation of this study was carried out and delivered in the first half of 2024. I found myself contemplating the vastness

Preface

of God and His cosmic plan followed by the radical change He has called us to in our personal life. The depth and richness of this letter is inexhaustible with our finite intellect. Even though this letter has only six chapters, this turns out to be the longest study I have written to date. The first half is fast-paced and jam-packed with doctrinal truths which take time to unravel and handle. In the second half, applications touch on many issues of our day, each of which demands proper attention in its own right. With the limited space here, we can only afford a broad-brush approach to these issues. Even so, given the sweep of issues covered, it soon adds up. In delivering the live sessions, I opted to give more time for discussion and probe into the big issues of our day. Otherwise, our learning will remain academic and goes against Paul's intention for his readers. I take great pleasure in that group members who have been wrestling with Paul's teaching on women feel encouraged by seeing the controversy set in context and, for this reason, in a fresh light.

Therefore, this study contains more materials than you can possibly deliver in a group setting; this is intentional to provoke your thinking. Quotations from the original sources and references are also cited to help you, the leader, better trace the development of thoughts. The target is your understanding. This is designed to be an aid, not a replacement, for your preparation. You still need to tailor-make the delivery of the sessions to suit your group. To facilitate group study, a corresponding member's study guide (with questions only) is published separately.

May the God of our Lord Jesus Christ, the Father of glory, give you a knowledge of Him, having the eyes of your hearts enlightened, that you may know the mystery so revealed and the richness of our unimaginable inheritance in heaven, filling you with unspeakable joy to the brim and resolve to do every good work in His power.

Eunice Kwok
July 2024

A prayer

My Father is working until now and I am working (John 5:17).

Our Father in Heaven,

We give thanks that You have never abandoned Your creation but are working always to hold all things together. People may scorn Your name but they know not how our lives would have disintegrated if not for You and Your grace. The signature of Your works is order, whether it is in the physical world or in human morality. Where Your law is abandoned, we see the latter decay into disorder. We see much darkness in ourselves and in the world had not for Your grace to shine light into our minds and our life. Let us, O Lord, marvel and praise together how this light broke into history and awakened corrupt souls from deadness like dry bones restored back to life in the first century. As we study this miraculous transformation You instigated, we know we do not need that powerful gospel work any less today. O Lord, work in us, we pray. O Lord, come and teach us, as we gather round Your word in order that we may praise and glorify Your name. May the Spirit speak to each of us directly now, renewing our minds and helping us live it out in our life, to the glory of Your name.

In Your Son's victorious name we pray, Amen.

1. An Overview [1:1-2]

*A*nd *Paul and Barnabas spoke out boldly, saying, "It was necessary that the word of God be spoken first to you. Since you thrust it aside and judge yourselves unworthy of eternal life, behold, we are turning to the Gentiles. For so the Lord has commanded us, saying,*
  'I have made you a light for the Gentiles,
  that you may bring salvation to the ends of the earth.'"
And when the Gentiles heard this, they began rejoicing and glorifying the word of the Lord, and as many as were appointed to eternal life believed. And the word of the Lord was spreading throughout the whole region (Acts 13:46-49).

Paul was *an apostle to the Gentiles* (Rom. 11:13).

Paul in Ephesus

Read Acts 18-20.

1. **What were Paul's ties with the church in Ephesus?** Paul first took the gospel to Ephesus during his second missionary journey after his stops at Philippi, Thessalonica, Athens, and

Corinth. As he customarily did, he brought the gospel to the Jews first, going into the synagogue and reasoning with them (Acts 18:19). He did not stay long but moved on while leaving his companions, Priscilla and Aquila, there. Meanwhile, Apollo, a Jew, arrived and spoke boldly about Jesus. Yet his knowledge of the gospel was deficient in that *he knew only the baptism of John* (Acts 18:25), which was the baptism of repentance. Priscilla and Aquila took on the task of helping him understand the gospel of Christ more fully. Apollo later moved across to Achaia, being used powerfully by God for the cause of *the Way*. Paul later returned to Ephesus (Acts 19:1), encountering some who were baptized only into John's baptism (Acts 19:3). It probably reflected the deficiency of Apollo's initial teaching in the city. In face of the hostile reception of the gospel in the synagogue, Paul focused his time on training his disciples by reasoning with them daily (Acts 19:9). He stayed for over two years. His unusually long stay made Ephesus a centre for evangelising the western part of Asia Minor (Acts 19:10). A major political uproar broke out against *the Way* (Acts 19:23), and soon afterwards, Paul left Ephesus to continue his journey as guided by the Spirit. On his way back to Jerusalem, he made a stop at Miletus, where he gathered the elders of the church in Ephesus to see them one last time. Paul's reflection of his ministry there and his affectionate ties with the church can be seen in his moving farewell speech to the elders of the church (Acts 20:17-38).

2. **What can we gather about the city Ephesus?** With its location, Ephesus was the capital of the Roman province of Asia on the west coast of Asia Minor (today's Turkey). First-century Ephesus was the richest city in the most prosperous province of the Roman Empire and unsurprisingly it also boasted a large population. It was a Gentile pagan city, worshipping the goddess of Diana (or known by its Greek

Session 1: Ephesians 1:1-2

name Artemis).[3] The city housed the Temple of Diana, so magnificent in size and architecture that it was one of the Seven Wonders of the Ancient World. Measuring two hundred and twenty-five feet by four hundred and twenty-five feet, the temple of Diana dominated the city and its civic life. One inscription describes the city as the 'nurturer' of the goddess and in turn the goddess made it the 'more glorious' of the Asian cities. Ephesus and the cult of Diana were inseparable. It was not surprising that pagan worship supported commerce in the city. As believers purged its practice from their lives following conversion, trade suffered and it stirred up hostile opposition, nearly causing a riot in the city (see Acts 19:11ff).

3. **Based on answer to Q2, what kinds of challenges do you imagine new believers faced in Ephesus?** Given the background of the city, it means that the gospel was extremely counter-cultural in Ephesus at the time. Inward transformation by the power of the gospel necessarily has its outward expressions in behaviour. The believers of the early church would have been the minority. They were likely to be marginalised in a pluralistic society, which was tolerant of many things but not the gospel of Christ as it was proven too radical and caused an upheaval to their way of life. For the believers to stand firm in an ungodly society and not to be carried away by every wind of fad, their conviction must be strong and their identity secure in Christ. Paul wrote the letter to encourage them, reminding them of the solid and unshakable foundation of their new identity, from which a

---

[3] 'Apollo is held to be the prophet and the healer; yet the pagans were determined to locate him in some part of the world, so they said that he was the sun. And his sister Diana was the moon and the goddess in charge of roads – hence they insisted that she was a virgin, because a road is unproductive. The reason why these two carry arrows is that those two stars extend their rays from the sky to the earth' (St. Augustine, City of God, translated by Henry Bettenson, Penguin (2003), p.273).

new lifestyle and a church family sprang. When the going got tough, Paul asked them to <u>remember</u> who they were.

4. **What was Paul's admonition to the church in his farewell speech to the elders (Acts 20:28-32)?** Paul warned them it was a constant battle against the enemy, who would send fierce wolves to come in among them and from among them would arise false teachers speaking twisted things and drawing away disciples. They, as the appointed overseers, must be alert and on guard as always, paying careful attention to themselves and to all the flock entrusted to them. He did not leave them without defence. He reminded them *the word of his grace, which is able to build you up and to give you the inheritance among all those who are sanctified* (Acts 20:32). We may see this as an introduction to Paul's letter to the Ephesians which continues the theme set out here.

The Salutation

Read Ephesians 1:1-2. In Paul's time, the cultural traditions were to open a letter with the names of both the writer and the recipient, followed by some words of greetings. Paul employs the customarily format in almost all of his letters and adapts it with the gospel truths.

5. **Who is the writer of the letter and how does he introduce himself?** Paul is the writer. Paul was not the name he had always been known for. The name change from Saul to Paul is recorded in Acts 13:9: *But Saul, who was also called Paul ...* at the beginning of the Antioch Church's outreach mission. Paul was from the tribe of Benjamin, a Hebrew of Hebrews (Phil. 3:5). His hometown was Tarus, a cosmopolitan city. He might have been given two names from birth. Anyhow, the context of his name change suggests that it might be for the sake of his leadership of the mission to the Gentiles. From then on, he

Session 1: Ephesians 1:1-2

came to be known by 'Paul', which was less obviously Jewish than 'Saul'.

He introduces himself as *an apostle of Christ Jesus by the will of God*. The Greek word *apostolos* means 'a sent one'. His authority to speak and act depends on the nature of his sender. Therefore he specifies that he was an apostle *of Christ Jesus*. Paul often emphasised that he was commissioned directly by the Lord Jesus Himself, just like Peter or John, lest his calling was demeaned and his authority under attack. Furthermore he was called *by the will of God*. The emphasis is important to establish the source of his authority in speaking on behalf of God to the church. By doing so, he states why he should be listened to as opposed to the false teachers whom he has warned them about.

6. **Who were the original recipients of the letter and how did Paul address them?** The letter was written *to the saints who are in Ephesus, and are faithful in Christ Jesus*. According to the New Testament, all believers are *saints*, not by years of hard effort to perfection but by their status as being 'set apart' for God's special purpose, gained from their spiritual resurrection and transformation when they first believe and trust in Christ as their personal Saviour. Becoming holy is the natural fruit of becoming a saint; the inward transformation will have its outward manifestation. The saints are characterised by their two locations: *in Ephesus* and *in Christ Jesus*. They have citizenship in heaven while they reside on earth (in Ephesus) as pilgrims. Being *faithful* is a response to God's grace. However, Christ gives His assessment of the church in Ephesus in Revelation 2:1-7. While they remained faithful in defending the gospel truth against falsehood, Christ held one thing against them: *you have abandoned the love you had at first* and called them to repent or *I will come to you and remove the lampstand from your place*. They had grown to be

a loveless church. Trials in Christian walk are plenty and our faithfulness depends on God's faithfulness.

7. **What is Paul's greeting to the recipients of the letter?** *Grace to you and peace from God our Father and the Lord Jesus Christ.* Writing with the apostolic authority, Paul wishes them nothing less than grace and peace from both the Father and the Son. Grace is the underserved love of God lavished on us which is the fountain of all blessings. Peace is equivalent to *Shalom* in Hebrew, which has complex meanings, covering spiritual prosperity and completeness, which can only be found in God. In putting the Father and the Son side by side, Paul acknowledges their equality.

8. **When did Paul write the letter (3:1, 4:1, 6:20)?** Paul wrote this letter when he was a prisoner in chain. We cannot be absolutely sure where Paul was imprisoned when he wrote the letter, but the traditional setting is that Paul wrote it from prison in Rome around AD 60-62, which remains the most likely place. Paul seems to have written four letters from prison at that time: Ephesians, Philippians, Colossians, and Philemon. During his final imprisonment, he wrote to Ephesus again but this time more personal letters to Timothy. Prior to that, he was imprisoned in other places. Although Paul was in chain, the gospel was not in chain; although his body was confined, his soul soared freely like an eagle to the lofty praise of God! Such is the power and joy of the gospel that the soul has been set free and it is free indeed.

Because the phrase *in Ephesus* (1:1) is not in many early manuscripts, many scholars think that the letter was a circular to more than one congregation. Paul sent Tychicus to them (6:21-22); he might have carried several copies of this letter and left a copy to each church he visited in Asia Minor. It may be that it was first sent to Ephesus and that was why the letter became especially associated with the city. Ferguson sums it up well: 'Thinking of it as a circular letter certainly makes sense of both its style and its contents. But whether or not it was so in the first century Asia, it is a circular to the whole church of Jesus Christ today!'[4] Its relevance to today's churches never wanes due to the passing of time.

The Structure of the Letter

Read through the letter and you will see that Ephesians is a letter of two halves.

9. **What is the relationship between the two halves?** It is obvious that Chapters 1-3 forms one block and Chapters 4-6 forms another. The first half is on doctrine while the second half on behaviour; the first half is theological while the second half practical. This is shown by the fact that there are no imperatives in the first half, except one which is 'to remember' what we once were and no longer (2:11), while the second half is full of imperatives. The first half focuses on what God has already done for us in Christ (verbs in indicative mood), which forms the basis of everything Paul urges us to do (imperatives) in the second half. Our godly living reflects our love for God as a response to what God has done for us. That is, the power of the gospel propels our all-life worship in obedience. The two parts are inseparable. If the imperatives are cut off from the indicatives, we will be fulfilling them in our own strength rather than through the gospel power. If we observe the commands without the love for God, it will become legalistic. Another way of saying the same thing is that the first half describes what it means to be *in Christ* while the second half what it means to live that out *in Ephesus*, an ungodly culture. As the second half expresses

---

[4] Ferguson, Sinclair (2005) *Let's Study Ephesians*, The Banner of Truth, p. xiv

the character of God and His love for us, our understanding is rooted in the first half. The letter therefore is tightly woven together.

Applications

10. If you are a believer, are you surprised being called 'a saint'? Explain.

11. What is your surrounding culture? In what ways do the challenges of the believers in Ephesus resonate with yours in your daily life?

Session 1: Ephesians 1:1-2

12. Who do you listen to in life? How do you choose? Is the advice you receive 'good' or 'bad'? How do you judge?

2. A Cascade of Blessings [1:3-14]

How do you convey a breathtaking view of God? By constructing a sentence that will physically take your breath away when you read it out! Almost every commentary you read on Ephesians will tell you the same thing about today's passage, that the whole segment is one long, unbroken sentence in Greek, stretching to over two hundred words! It was as though Paul could not but cascade God's blessings in one breath to maximise its dramatic impact that should overwhelm us with awe and wonder, and in turn draw us into the chorus of praise to God. Anchoring our faith and identity in the riches of divine grace is how we stand firm in an ungodly society without being shaken and infested with doubt.

In this panoramic view of God's salvation plan for us, Paul stretches our minds to see that from eternity past, we were chosen by God the Father to be redeemed by the blood of our Lord Jesus Christ in the present and sealed by the Holy Spirit for our inheritance as sons in eternity future. In one long sentence, Paul maps out the unmovable purpose of God's will from *before the foundation of the world* and magnificently displays our

Session 2: Ephesians 1:3-14

salvation plan as a Trinitarian work whereby the Father, the Son and the Holy Spirit work in harmony and unison. Now hold tight, and let's go under the cascade and be showered by the spiritual blessings in abundance!

Self-reflective Question

Who are you? What is the identity that most defines you? What does it build on?

Our Election (1:3-6a)

1. **How does God bless us and how do we bless God (1:3)?** If earthly parents bless their children with the best they can give them, our heavenly Father is infinitely greater. He is *the* source of all good things; there is no other source of goodness except from Him. *Every good gift and every perfect gift is from above, coming down from the Father of lights* (Jas. 1:17). *If you then, who are evil, know how to give good gifts to your children, how much more will your Father who is in heaven give good things to those who ask him* (Matt. 7:11)! God is the supreme Blesser, because He alone is good and in turn alone bestows upon us *every* spiritual blessing (verse 3).

It is harder to think how we may bless God. It is a frequent command in the Psalms, for example: *Bless the LORD, O my soul, and all that is within me, bless his holy name .... Blessed be the God* (Ps. 103:1, 3). 'Bless' here means 'to speak well' of someone. 'From *eulogeō* (blessed) we get eulogy, a message of praise and commendation, the declaration of a person's goodness. Because no one is truly good but God (Matt. 19:17), our supreme eulogy, our supreme praise, is for Him alone.'[5] In face of His great goodness, the only right response from us is to praise and *bless His name*!

2. **Where is the location of these spiritual blessings and what is the source of them (1:3)? How do these spiritual blessings stand in contrast to the blessing of Moses?** Spiritual blessings are immaterial with its source from the Spirit, impacting on our inner being rather than outward fortunes. Verse 3 announces the age of the New Covenant, marking the departure from the Law of Moses, the Old Covenant, which offered earthly promises. Instead, the New Covenant has come into being through Christ Jesus, and in His perfection the kingdom of heaven is promised, offering eternal blessedness, of which the temporal (or earthly) blessings were a shadow. While it is the design of God that the earth is filled through <u>reproduction</u> in the Creation order, citizens of the heavenly kingdom are recruited by <u>regeneration</u>, through the remission of sins in Christ Jesus. Therefore, <u>Christ, and only *in Christ* (v1 cf. v4, v6b), is the source of every spiritual blessing</u>.

These blessings are *in the heavenly places*, which refer to the new realm of spiritual realities into which believers have been brought in Christ. From its usage elsewhere in this

---

[5] MacArthur, John (1986), *The MacArthur New Testament Commentary on Ephesians*, Moody Publishers, p. 7.

Session 2: Ephesians 1:3-14

epistle (in 1:20, 2:6, 3:10 and 6:12), *the heavenly places* encompass God's complete domain and the full extent of His divine operation. They are not future realities after our death but are our present realities wherever Christ is enthroned and His name is honoured through faith – notably in believers' hearts and lives and in His Church. *For behold, the kingdom of God is in the midst of you* (Luke 17:21). As highlighted by Paul in the salutation (1:1), faithful saints are simultaneously in two locations: *in Ephesus* and *in Christ* (see Session 1 Q6). The spiritual realm concerns things unseen, brought to us by the conviction of our faith. *A man's steps are from the* LORD*; how then can man understand his way?* This is a very good question from Proverbs 20:24. As we enter *the heavenly places*, we gain the unseen insight and understanding of things that are seen, to help us navigate our life on earth with wisdom from the LORD. The key to living as a heavenly citizen in this sin-cursed world is walking by the Spirit.

3. **How did God the Father will this to happen (1:4-6a)?**
   - *He chose us before the foundation of the world.* The very time when the election took place means that we could not have done anything to merit it.
   - This election is *in him* (i.e. in Christ). If it is in Christ, it is not of ourselves and excludes all our merits. Rather, it is in the merit of Christ.
   - God did this *according to the purpose of his will* (v5). It means that His will is the first cause, that the origin of our faith does not lie with us but with God's action, God's purpose and God's will. It is His divine free grace from start to finish and we play no part in His sovereign election.

Application: What are the difficulties in us accepting the doctrine of election?

- Our nature inclines us to a work-based salvation: that God has chosen me must be for a reason about me, that I have done something right. This doctrine eliminates that completely, *so that no one may boast* (2:9b). It is all God (His will, His purpose, His love) and nothing about us, that all glory be to Him (v6a).
- Most people believe that we have 'free will'. We have 'free will' only as far as we have a will and we are free to choose without coercion. Just as we can't get the house we like because it is outside our budget, some choices are simply not available to us because of our inability. The spectrum of choices available to us is restricted. The Bible teaches that we are captive to sin and are by nature at enmity with God (cf. Rom. 8:7-8). Left on our own devices, we will never seek or desire God (Rom. 3:11). Jonathan Edwards distinguishes between natural and moral inability. It is not that we lack rational faculties or bodily powers but the proclivity to choose God due to our moral aversion. We are described as being dead in our trespasses and sins (2:1). We need to be set free from that bondage if we are ever going to desire Christ.
- We tend to argue that if God sovereignly chooses whom to save, it is unfair or unjust to hold human responsible for their unbelief. For many, this is a stumbling block for it shows that God is unreasonable. The position of the Bible is that God's sovereign election and human responsibility are parallel truths, which our finite mind with its logic has difficulty in reconciling. However, I find it helpful to consider the conflict in this way: God's justice demands damnation for all and does not obligate God to save any. The fact that He saves some is out of His mercy, which by definition is not owed to us at all. It is God's prerogative to choose whom He is going to save – because He is God!

Session 2: Ephesians 1:3-14

This is a stark reminder: 'Demand justice (as Portia in Shakespeare's *The Merchant of Venice* saw so clearly) and I am lost and damned:

> *Though justice be thy plea, consider this*
> *That, in the course of justice, none of us*
> *Should see salvation: we do pray for mercy.*'[6]

4. **Who are the chosen ones predestined to be (1:5)? What does it mean to you?** The chosen ones are predestined *for adoption as sons through Jesus Christ*. We often take this for granted that we miss being awestruck and completely gobsmacked by this great and glorious spiritual blessing of ours! A judge who acquits you in the courtroom is not obligated to bring you home and adopt you as his son. Justification and adoption go hand in hand in God's salvation plan for us not because of necessity or some prior logic but because it is the expression of God's character, that He is the Father Almighty. Let us take a moment to allow this extraordinary and astounding privilege to sink in.

Before God was the Creator, He was the Father, as revealed by His Son. Fatherhood is the deepest revelation of the identity of God: He *is* the Father. If we only know God as the Creator and not the Father, we are damned; this is precisely the problem of sinners. If we do not know God as the Father, we do not know God properly. To be a father is to beget life and love his son. This is revealed by how God loves and delights in His Son perfectly from eternity past. This identity of God as the Father entirely shapes the gospel. His plan before the foundation of the world is to have His chosen ones who have rejected Him to be brought back to Him through the forgiveness of sins in Christ, not as mere creatures but as

---

[6] Ferguson, Sinclair, ibid., p. 9, quoting from Shakespeare's *The Merchant of Venice*, Act IV, Scene I.

His children. <u>Adoption is the height of our privilege, as it gives us Sonship, having the access and enjoying the abounding love Christ has always known of His Father.</u> Jesus prays His priestly prayer for His own: *Father, I desire that they also, whom you have given me, may be with me where I am, to see my glory that you have given me because you loved me before the foundation of the world* (John 17:24). That we should partake in that should blow our minds away. Christ is in the bosom of God the Father and He wants us to be where He is! <u>Salvation is better and more secure than forgiveness of sins.</u> Through the Spirit of adoption, we cry out 'Abba, Father' as Christ does, and we love Christ as His Father does. Christ is not ashamed to call us His brothers (Heb. 2:11). Adoption is not based on performance – nothing we can do to earn the Sonship! It is all divine grace and how rich it is![7]

5. **What are we to be transformed into (1:4b)? What is the ultimate goal (1:6a)?** *That we should be holy and blameless before him* (v4b) is the same standing as Christ before God which has been given us in Christ. While our position is secure in our salvation, our practice can and does always fall short. We are certainly not chosen because we are holy but we are chosen *for good works* (2:10), to become holy and blameless. We will grow into the substance of what our status suggests. Being embraced into God's royal family and immersed in a love so lavish and complete cannot leave us unchanged. Our holiness however is not the ultimate goal. The highest end of our salvation is *to the praise of his glorious name* (v6a).

---

[7] Based on Michael Reeves, Session 2: *God, the Father Almighty*, at We Believe: 2024 Winter Conference, Ligonier Ministries, 19 January 2024.

Session 2: Ephesians 1:3-14

Our Redemption (1:7-10)

6. **What is a mystery in bible language (1:9)?** 'In the Old Testament is the New Testament concealed; the New Testament is the Old Testament revealed' (Augustine). *The secret things belong to the LORD our God, but the things that are revealed belong to us and to our children for ever, that we may do all the words of this law* (Deut. 29:29). A mystery in bible language refers to a secret that can be known only when God reveals it. The Bible is a progressive revelation of God's purpose and will. God has been single-minded on His plan since before the foundation of the world, but He did not reveal everything He wanted us to know in one go. Therefore, in the Old Testament, we had revelations that hinted at Christ. When Christ is here, what once was hidden as a mystery is now made known; they are *things into which angels long to look* (1 Pet. 1:12).

7. **What is the revealed mystery of God's will (1:8, 10)? What is the implication for us?** God has this ultimate plan, in the fullness of time, *to unite all things in Christ, things in heaven and things on earth.* It suggests that things are currently scattered rather than unified, fragmented and broken rather than coherent. After the Fall, the world is cursed by sin. Disintegration and disorder are facts of life that we only know too well. Outside Christ is only disorder. God has a plan to reintegrate the cosmos *in Christ*, to restore the paradise lost in Adam. As the proper condition of creatures is to keep close to God, a *gathering up together* will bring us back to the divine order, and God's plan is to accomplish this feat *in Christ*. When will this happen? God runs His plan according to His own timetable. He is never late; when *the fullness of time* arrives, we can be sure that His will be done. In the meantime we need to wait in patience with unswerving confidence in the certainty of God's purpose.

'Heaven and earth' means the whole of creation, material as well as spiritual. Here is the question that Calvin asks in his commentary: why are heavenly beings included in the number as the angels were never separated from God, and cannot be said to have been scattered? Just as a building in need of repairs does not rule out parts that are intact, the ruinous human race is restored and united in harmony with the celestial beings, all under Christ. Calvin however has his own view: 'Men had been lost, and angels were not beyond the reach of danger. By *gathering* both into his own body, Christ hath united them to God the Father, and established actual harmony between heaven and earth.'

8. **What is the means by which God accomplishes His plan (1:7)?** We are all captives of sin and need redemption to be set free. To be restored to God as His people, we need *forgiveness of our trespasses*. Moses led Israelites out of Egypt, delivering them from slavery. Similarly, Jesus leads His people in a new exodus out of the bondage, not to Pharaoh but to sin. This price for our redemption from sin was paid by Christ's death on the cross, in order that we may be united *in Him*. Our redemption is *in Christ, through his blood*, a metonym of death, the penalty and the price of sin. What motivated the plan? Nothing but the riches of God's grace (v7), which *he lavished upon us, in all wisdom and insight* (v8). God the Father is generous in His giving towards His children, grace we already have in Christ.

Our inheritance (1:11-14)

9. **Who are *we* in 1:11-12?** *We* in verses 11 and 12 denote the Jews, as Paul was. This is as opposed to *you also* in verse 13, which denotes the Gentiles being brought into God's

salvation plan through hearing the gospel of Christ and believing in Him. *We were the blessed people who were the first to hope in Christ* because God spoke to them of Christ through the prophets.

10. **What did *we* observe (1:11)?** The Jews observed God work through the long history to bring to fruition the salvation plan He had promised. They testified His steadfast love and faithfulness to His people as they recognised Christ as the fulfilment of God's prophecy. There were Old Testament saints who put their faith in the Old Testament promise (Heb. 11). That God is the One who *works all things according to the counsel of his will* (v11) is probably the strongest statement of His absolute sovereignty in the whole of Bible. It is not sufficient that God makes plan but that He also makes it work out. It speaks of God as the sole agent of doing everything according to His will, admitting no men to share in this praise. God pursuing His own glory is not at our expense; to the contrary, it brings us greatest happiness (or felicity)! Witnessing God's will being unfolded in history and become the reality of the saints speaks of the splendour and majesty of God. They *might be to the praise of his glory* (v12), i.e. they eventually become the illustrations of the glory of God in His display cabinet. Nothing is outside His sovereign control, even with things that baffle us. May this give us peace and confidence in all circumstances that surpass all understanding! Amen.

11. **How are the Gentiles brought into the fold of God's people (1:13)?** The Gentiles did not have prophets or the promise to hope in. In the New Testament, they are saved through hearing the word of truth, the gospel of Christ and believe in Him (v13). Such is the power in the gospel, it is not surprising that Satan's usual scheme is to discredit and ridicule the gospel, leading us either to doubt or to despise it. In Romans,

Paul describes the Gentiles as if they were wild olive shoots being grafted into the olive tree and supported by its root (Rom. 11:17). They have the same mark of being *sealed with the promised Holy Spirit* (v13), rather than by any authority of men. In the ancient world, the seal was usually made from hot wax placed on a document which was then impressed with a signet ring. <u>It provided security, authenticity, ownership and authority.</u> Paul is stressing that believers, Jews or Gentiles, have the same seal, which is the promised Spirit of God Himself to remove any doubt and sustain our hope: the seal of security of their salvation, authenticity of their faith, God's ownership and their authority to proclaim the good news of Christ.

12. **What is the shared inheritance (1:11, 14)?** In verse 11, Paul talks about the Jews obtaining an inheritance, and in verse 14, he talks about the guarantee of *our* inheritance – that of Jews and Gentiles. *For there is no distinction between Jew and Greek; for the same Lord is Lord of all, bestowing his riches on all who call on him. For "everyone who calls on the name of the Lord will be saved"* (Rom. 10:12-13). Jews and Gentiles have the <u>same</u> inheritance, which encompass all the extraordinary blessings and exclusive privileges from their adoption as sons through Jesus Christ (see Q4), <u>heirs to eternal life.</u>

Summary

13. **List the spiritual blessings discussed.** God's glorious grace in election, adoption (sonship), redemption, forgiveness of sins, unity with Christ, the indwelling of the Holy Spirit as the seal, spiritual illumination, and inheritance.

14. **'Our redemption is the work of the Blessed Trinity.' How do we see this doctrinal truth in today's passage?** The focus of verses 3-6 is God the Father, that of verses 7-10 is Jesus

Session 2: Ephesians 1:3-14

Christ the Son, and that of verses 11-14 is the Holy Spirit. In other words, our redemption is planned by the Father, accomplished by the Son, and applied by the Holy Spirit. The activity of all three persons in the Trinity is needed to redeem us.

'The salvation in which Paul glories is itself a revelation of God's glory as Father, Son and Holy Spirit. It has taken the energies of the whole Godhead to bring to us the blessing of grace! Each divine person is equally necessary to our enjoyment of these blessings; each person is united in purpose and will with the other persons in order that we might be redeemed.'[8]

Applications

15. What kind of God do you see behind the doctrine of sovereign election: unfair and unreasonable or the most gracious and worthy of the highest praise? What are your struggles with it or how have you overcome them?

---

[8] Ferguson, Sinclair, ibid., p. 20.

If you are struggling with the doctrine of sovereign election, take heart that you are not alone. It is so alien to our nature that we cannot grasp it on our own effort; we need the Spirit's inspiration to authenticate it in our hearts. Do not give up but persevere in your understanding with a submissive heart to God's truth. Pray for wisdom and insight to see it. You may have to ask your pastor or spiritual mentor on the subject. Alternatively, you can turn to books expounding the doctrines of grace. Trust me, it is worth wrestling with it as from it flows abundant spiritual blessing: security, assurance, peace and rest.

16. What is your relationship with God? Do you know God as the Father? How has your understanding of your sonship – the extent of how much God has loved you – impacted you? Say a prayer of confession and/or thanksgiving.

17. How has today's study encouraged you in your faith walk?

18. Look back to the self-reflective question at the start. Has your answer changed or been refined after the study? Have you discovered something new about your identity in Christ? If so, what is it?

3. Lack no Good Thing [1:15-23]

Oh, taste and see that the LORD is good! Blessed is the man who takes refuge in him! Oh, fear the LORD, you his saints, for those who fear him have no lack! The young lions suffer want and hunger; but those who seek the LORD lack no good thing (Ps. 34:8-10). From this study, we see that Paul wants to get this truth to sink in and impact our life, that we, who are saints in Christ, lack no good thing! Alleluia!

Self-reflective Questions

How would you describe your prayer life? Is prayer your first or last resort? Do you pray occasionally, or habitually? Are you a prayer warrior?

Session 3: Ephesians 1:15-23

What dominate the contents of your prayer?

What structure of prayer, if any, do you follow in practice and why?

Motivation to Pray (1:15-16)

1. **This section starts with** *for this reason* **(1:15). What motivates Paul to pray?** In one breath and huge excitement, Paul has just finished taking us on this grand tour of God's revealed purpose and will of calling a people for His own possession in Christ, with a panoramic vision stretching from eternity past to eternity future. With 1:3-14, Paul wants to strike home that God's grace has made us immeasurably rich with every spiritual blessing in Christ: election, pre-destination, adoption, redemption, forgiveness, the seal of the promised Holy Spirit and an inheritance. Once hidden as a

mystery of His will is now revealed – that God has a plan in motion to unite all things in Him in the fullness of time – and all these riches are already in believers' possession. Paul is moved to pray for believers, that these riches will take full effect and yield fruit in their life.

2. **Given that Paul was in prison, what had kept him informed (1:15)?** It had been about four years since Paul ministered in Ephesus. But he 'heard' news from letters or from personal friends who visited him and brought him reports. He therefore had received considerable information from and about the churches. It also supports that this might have been a 'circular' letter to the region and not specifically written to Ephesus.

3. **What are the marks that Paul notes about the saints and why are they significant (1:15)?** Paul notes two marks of his readers: their *faith in the Lord Jesus* and their *love towards all the saints*. The genuine marks of conversion and in turn transformed lives are believers' vertical relationship with God and their horizontal relationships with others, especially their fellow believers.

While they had kept their faith pure and persevered in it, sadly their love became lackluster as time went by. In His letters to the seven churches, Jesus held this against the Ephesians, *that you had abandoned the love you had at first* (Rev 2:4). The great love for Christ and for all the saints that Paul had praised warmly just a few decades earlier was lost. It shows that Christians must be always on guard (Mark 13:23) as Christ has commanded, and prayer is an important strategy!

4. **How does Paul show his love to his readers (1:16)?** Prayer is love. If you doubt that, pray for someone you dislike for 30

consecutive days and see if your heart is changed. Paul did not have difficulty in praying for his readers as he was so fond of them: *I do not cease to give thanks for you, remembering you in my prayers.* Knowing the impossibility of us turning to Christ on our own devices, Paul marvelled at every believer as a walking miracle of God's divine grace. Remembering his own miraculous conversion, Paul never forgot whom to thank for the fruit-bearing faith in his readers. He was so awestruck by the wonder and power of God's grace that he was always bent to thanksgiving. His constant and fatherly interest in them sustained a prayer effort that was consistent, mirroring the steadfastness of God's love.

Application: Are you giving thanks to God unceasingly in your prayer life?

Is prayer the true evidence of love in your church life? How intentional are you in praying for others? Do you find your *love towards all the saints* grow when you sincerely intercede for them?

5. **Look back to Session 1. What practical difficulties do you think Paul's readers faced in their Christian walk?** Their main challenge was to stand firm in faith in the midst of an ungodly city which readily made known her violent opposition to the gospel when the people felt their way of life

was threatened (Acts 19:21ff). Christians in Ephesus and the region were likely to be marginalised and ostracised, suffering socially and financially for the name of Christ.

6. **Why does Paul pray in lofty terms rather than specific difficulties his readers faced? Can his prayer be more relevant to their life?** It is an example of a spiritual leader to be concerned about the spiritual growth of those in his care. Paul's prayer lifts our eyes up heavenward, pleading that believers <u>know</u> the greatness of the hope, the power and Christ the person. He did not pray in these lofty terms because he lacked knowledge of the practical difficulties and personal circumstances of his readers; after all, he had lived in Ephesus for at least two years and knew the church there intimately. Nor did he pray in these lofty and general terms because it was a circular letter. Instead, his prayer cuts to the chase and addresses the fundamental issue of <u>ineffectiveness</u> in believers, which makes standing firm in faith a daily struggle more than it needs to be. It is like we Christians each have a limitless bank account in our names already. Having no knowledge or understanding of how richly endowed we are stops us from drawing on it, especially in time of needs. Rather than being irrelevant, Paul with his spiritual sight goes higher and stretches farther that our fundamental need to see our privileges will be met; 'for unless we see how great they are we will neither desire to enter into them fully nor will we be able to live in the light of them.'[9] <u>We think we are poor not because God is insufficient to our needs but because our sight is limited.</u> Paul's prayer is to correct the latter so that we may see how God has already opened a floodgate of blessings to cascade down on us.

---

[9] Ferguson, Sinclair, ibid., p. 24.

Session 3: Ephesians 1:15-23

What to pray (1:17-23)

7. **The genius of this prayer is that it is timeless and for all situations. What is Paul's petition to God for believers (1:17-18a)?** Paul petitions God to give believers a comprehension and appreciation of their true and full identity in Christ Jesus. Our problem is not a lack of blessings but a lack of knowledge to understand and use them properly and faithfully. *For my thoughts are not your thoughts, neither are your ways my ways, declares the* LORD. *For as the heavens are higher than the earth, so are my ways higher than your ways and my thoughts than your thoughts* (Isa. 55:8-9). We are unfit to receive the elevated knowledge of God! Therefore, *the knowledge of him* is not something that we can gain by ourselves but something to be given to us by *the God of our Lord Jesus Christ, the Father of glory* through *a spirit of wisdom and of revelation*, hence the petition.

Calvin explains the meaning of *the God of our Lord Jesus Christ*: 'The Son of God became man in such a manner, that God was his God as well as ours.' The title *the Father of glory* springs from this that 'God's glory, as a Father, consists in subjecting his Son to our condition, that through him, he might be our God.'[10]

God's blessings to us are so rich that we rely on *a spirit of wisdom and revelation* given to us for our understanding. *Revelation* does not mean our own private revelation but the Spirit's *illumination* to us of what God has already revealed about Himself in Christ and through the Spirit. Often, *a spirit of wisdom* is interpreted to be the Holy Spirit. However, MacArthur argues that 'Believers already possess the Holy Spirit (Rom. 8:9), for whom their bodies are temples (1 Cor.

---

[10] Calvin's commentary on Ephesians, available online.

6:19)... But like our English *spirit*, *pneuma* sometimes was used of a disposition, influence or attitude ... Paul prayed for God to give the Ephesians a special disposition of **wisdom**, the fullness of godly knowledge and understanding of which the sanctified mind is capable of receiving.'[11] Either interpretation means spiritual sight as if *the eyes of your hearts [were] enlightened* (v18a). Rather than being the seat of emotions and feelings, the *heart* in the New Testament refers to 'the centre of knowledge, understanding, thinking, and wisdom... The heart was considered to be the seat of the mind and will, and it could be taught what the brain could never know.'[12]

8. **What are the three things that Paul prays for believers to know and understand (1:18b-19)?**
   - The hope of their divine call;
   - The riches of God's glorious inheritance in the saints; and
   - The immeasurable greatness of His power towards us who believe.

9. **How did the first two things relate to Paul's readers, who were Gentiles (see 2:12)?** Before their divine call, they had no hope and without God in the world (2:12). They did not enjoy the special covenantal relationship that God had with the Jews, so they did not have the hope of the Jews in their promises. A world without God is a hopeless business indeed! But now Gentiles have been called into God's kingdom: *faith comes from hearing, and hearing through the word of Christ* (Rom. 10:17); *of his own will he brought us forth by the word of truth* (Jas. 1:18). Now there is no distinction between Jews and Gentiles, who enjoy the same hope in Christ.

---

[11] MacAthur, John, ibid., p. 44.
[12] MacAthur, John, ibid., p. 45.

Session 3: Ephesians 1:15-23

Christian hope is not wishful thinking but certainty of the reality we are going to inherit in the future.

The riches of God's glorious inheritance in the saints could mean the people as God's inheritance, His 'treasured possession' (for example, Ps. 28:9, 33:12, 78:71, and Mal. 3:16-17) or God Himself as the people's inheritance. As one necessarily implies the other in the relationship, either interpretation makes sense of the text. But given the context, the focus weighs towards the riches we have as in 1:11 which refers to our blessings.

How do such realisations encourage the readers (including ourselves) to keep their faith? That we were chosen (and therefore wanted) before the foundation of the world gives us dignity and a sense of worthiness. That all things will work out according to God's good purpose and will gives us security as in God there is only certainty; what He says will come to pass (1:11). Believers suffer for the name of Christ. At Ephesus for example, believers walking away from the occult practice meant that they were likely to lose their income, influence and maybe even inheritance. Paul wants to put believers' suffering in the eternal perspective and renew their inner self in the midst of affliction: *For this light momentary affliction is preparing for us an eternal weight of glory beyond all comparison, as we look not to the things that are seen but to the things that are unseen. For the things that are seen are transient, but the things that are unseen are eternal* (2 Cor. 4:17-18). The riches awaiting us on the other side are *beyond all comparison*! Like Paul himself, it should be no brainer for us either to *count everything as loss because of the surpassing worth of knowing Christ Jesus my Lord* (Phil. 3:8).

10. **What might be the Ephesians' religious baggage from their pagan culture (cf. Jer. 44:17-18) that knowing 1:19 was especially reassuring?** Typically pagan gods are worshipped so that they might grant prosperity in this life. Life in Ephesus was dominated by the worship of Diana. If life had been going well before, it could be ingrained in people's mindset that bad fortunes after conversion to Christianity was caused by their abandonment of pagan worship. There might be ground for them to doubt, in the showdown of power and might, would God triumph over all? It is important for believers to appreciate *what is the immeasurable greatness of his power towards us who believe, according to the working of his great might* (v19); God is able to execute all His plan, so He is trustworthy to deliver the hope and the inheritance promised in verse 18.

11. **Where does Paul draw us to look as expressions of this immeasurable greatness of God's power (1:20-22)?** He draws our attention to the divine power that has worked in Christ,
    - in His resurrection (*when he raised him from the dead*),
    - in His ascension and exaltation (*seated him at his right hand in the heavenly places*), and
    - in His victory over all powers, now and forever, and in heaven and on earth (v21-22).

    What are the implications of these realities for our lives?
    - *But in fact Christ has been raised from the dead, the firstfruits of those who have fallen asleep* (1 Cor. 15:20). Resurrection is not resuscitation but an act of transformation, from our lowly bodies to be like His glorious one (Phil. 3:21). Although we have yet had our resurrected bodies, the resurrection power is already at work in us, transforming us into the new creation, enabling us to resist sins and having life over death.

Session 3: Ephesians 1:15-23

- Christ has been given all authority in heaven and on earth (Matt. 28:18). 'At the right hand' confers a position of honour; God has bestowed upon Christ the highest royal power to govern heaven and earth.

- With all the promises, it is important that they are underwritten by God's power which is greater than all (John 10:29). For their confidence, believers need to grasp that Christ's reign and authority is comprehensive across realms and is both temporal and eternal: it is *far above all rule and authority and power and dominion, and above every name that is named, not only in this age but also in the one to come* (v21). It means nothing and no powers, visible or invisible, material or spiritual, can thwart God's purpose (Job 42:2) or frustrate the advancement of Christ's kingdom. His promises are trustworthy, solid and unbreakable, so our hope is sure.

The implication is huge. God can say with confidence that *for those who love God all things work together for good... If God is for us, who can be against us? He who did not spare his own Son but gave him up for us all, how will he not also with him graciously give us all things? Who shall bring any charge against God's elect?* And nothing can separate us from the love of Christ! (Rom. 8:28, 31-33a, 39) He is in control even of the wicked: *The LORD has made everything for its purpose, even the wicked for the day of trouble* (Prov. 16:3). Martin Luther calls Christians 'the freest of kings,' arguing that 'every Christian by faith is exalted above all things. By virtue of the spiritual power provided in faith, a Christian is lord of all things and nothing is able to do him harm. It can even be said that all things are made subject to him and compelled to serve his salvation...'[13] What is Christ is ours. His power and dominion are such that He who is good will not permit evil to be done, were He not

---

[13] Martin Luther, *The Freedom of a Christian*, translated by Mark. D. Tranvik (2008), Fortress Press Minneapolis, p. 66.

omnipotent to bring good out of evil.[14]

12. **What is the applicatory climax of the above statement (1:22-23)?** *The* LORD *says to my Lord: "Sit at my right hand, until I make your enemies your footstool"* (Ps. 110:1). All things are put under Christ's feet and His headship over all things is such that He could save, protect and bless His people. The Church is called *his body* and Christ naturally cares for His own body. His reach and dominion *fill all in all*, meaning that there is nothing in the universe that does not belong to Him, and He rules all things for the sake of this body which is His fullness. <u>The glorious picture of Christ and His Church is this: Christ, in whom the fullness of God dwells, now dwells in His body (the Church), filling it up with His presence, flooding it with His love and grace, conforming it to His image until His likeness saturates it.</u> *For in him the whole fullness of deity dwells bodily, and you have been filled in him, who is the head of all rule and authority* (Col. 2:9-10).

Christ's excellence and beauty should dazzle our senses as incomprehensible and incomparable! Yet a head must have a body to manifest its glory, and Christ has chosen us, jars of clay, to manifest His glory as our Head and with us as His body. Calvin says, 'This is the highest honour of the church that until He is united to us, the Son of God reckons Himself in some measure incomplete. What consolation it is for us to learn that not until we are in His presence does He possess all His parts, nor does He wish to be regarded as complete.'[15]

---

[14] Calvin, *the Institutes of the Christian Religion*, translated by Henry Beveridge (2008) Hendrickson Publishers, 1:18:3.
[15] Quoted in MacArthur, John, ibid., p. 49.

Session 3: Ephesians 1:15-23

Applications

13. Look back to the self-reflective questions at the start. What can we learn from Paul for our private and corporate prayer?

14. Does your outlook of life reflect the reality that you are a victor in Christ? How has the knowledge of Christ reinforced or changed your outlook in life?

Whatever you are going through right now. I pray earnestly that you will hold your head up high with confidence as a victor in Christ.

15. How does today's study encourage you or a friend going through tough time, feeling lack? How does the knowledge of our richness in Christ answer your practical difficulties?

4. Zombies Come Alive [2:1-10]

Was there a season in your life when you felt like you were a zombie? A zombie is not formed when you have had a late night or two here and there, as a blip to your normal sleeping pattern that will soon be corrected. Rather, it is formed when chronic fatigue has seeped into your bone and marrow, weighing you down like lead to which you see no end. A zombie is someone going about his day without feeling or thinking. It is a shell performing what has been pre-programmed without engagement. Outwardly a zombie may look 'normal' but inwardly it is dead. Looking back, I was such a zombie when I was a working mum to infants for six years. The state of fatigue takes away your words to describe it; it is a state of existence that gives you no enjoyment. The endlessness of it darkens the horizon... This was not only my physical condition but also my spiritual state. It must be the greatest joy that life drives out death! Yet our senses have been dulled and we are robbed of our joy! Paul in today's text helps us see the miracle that has been accomplished in every believer, such that we may break out in doxology to God!

Paul starts the letter with a cascade of spiritual blessings which are ours in Christ. We see the beauty of how our redemption is the work of the triune God and how the work is already done and therefore our identity secure. The mystery of God's will is revealed that His plan is to unite all things in Christ in the fullness of time (1:10), things that are currently disordered, degenerated and disintegrated. Paul's prayer for believers is that we would truly and fully know the certainty of our hope, the richness of our inheritance and the greatness of God's power towards us (1:17-19). <u>Anchoring at these lofty truths is the secret of Christian walk.</u> Faith enables us to live out these future realities in the present, giving us the power to overcome the practical difficulties of this life.

In the verses immediately preceding today's passage, Paul shows us *the immeasurable greatness of God's power towards us who believe* (1:19) in Christ, enthroning Him as the King of all things. In today's session, we see that same power work the eternal plan of chapter 1 in our very own lives, making alive the walking dead. Had we seen a miracle, we would not have become tired of recounting it! Have we ever fully comprehended that each of us, saved and made alive together with Christ, is such miracle of God?

Self-reflective questions

In what ways do you understand your conversion as a miracle?

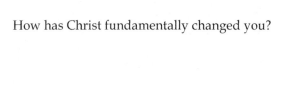

How has Christ fundamentally changed you?

Are you still regularly thanking God for your salvation?

Who we once were (2:1-3)

1. **Note the change in pronouns. Whom did verses 1-2 and verse 3 address respectively?** From Paul's perspective, verse 1-2 use the pronoun *you*, referring to the Gentiles. It switches to *we*, which refers to both Jews and Gentiles.

    What was the difference between Jews and Gentiles in the first century? What was the state of the Gentiles (2:1-2)? Unlike the Jews, Gentiles were not the recipient of the special covenant promises God had given to Abraham and his posterity. Neither did they have prophets through whom God spoke to them and guide their path. Instead, they were *strangers to the covenants of the promise, having no hope and without God in the world* (2:12). As such, they had only one way to live known to them, which was to *follow the course of the world* (v2). They therefore had a different *walk*, the

39

The Making of Living Stones

habitual manner in which they were used to live. They were *dead in the trespasses and sins* (v1). It does not mean that they were dead because they had committed sin but because they were in sin, referring to the state of existence of a person apart from God. It is not that we are sinners because we sin but that we sin because we are sinners. The word *trespasses* means 'to slip, fall, stumble, deviate, or go the wrong direction.'[16] The word *sin* means missing the mark.

2. **What is the world order that we were born to follow (2:2)?**
The course of this world is one that is against God and follows the leadership of Satan, *the prince of the power of the air*. Satan is the archenemy of God, a fallen angel who has rebelled against God. He is called *the deceiver of the whole world* (Rev. 12:9), *the god of this world* (2 Cor. 4:4), or *the father of lies* (John 8:44). However, he is no longer the ruler of the earth because he has been conquered by the risen Christ who now has all the authority in heaven and on earth given to Him (see Session 3 Q11). Satan first appeared in the Garden of Eden and tempted Eve, leading both Adam and Eve to sin. Now we were born in sin after the first Adam, he and his demon host work hard to keep us in their domain under their power, so that we would share their eternal fate of damnation. As a wanderer, Satan prowls around like a roaring lion, seeking someone to devour (1 Pet. 5:8). <u>He has an upper hand over us in that we in our sinful nature willingly fall for his schemes and deceptions.</u> They appeal to our nature and desire, centred on self-interest, self-importance, self-autonomy, self-aggrandisement and self-pleasure, all of which are music to our flesh. We therefore buy into current ideologies, such as humanism, expressive individualism, materialism, cultural Marxism, sexual liberation/ perversion / anarchy, narcissism on social-media,

---

[16] MacArthur, John, ibid., p.54.

Session 4: Ephesians 2:1-10

post-modernism and deconstructionism, just to name a few of the ongoing trends that have captivated our age. <u>Our rebellious spirit lies to us that breaking free from God, we are free!</u> The truth is that far from being free and independent, we are controlled by God's Enemy, who is a brutal, oppressive and evil master. Sin is indeed insanity when we believe we are better off hiding away from God to embrace Satan as our master.

3. **What does following the course of the world produce in us (2:2)?** It produces *sons of disobedience*. Hebrew idioms call *sinners* as sons of sin or a wealthy person as son of wealth. So *sons of disobedience* refer to persons characterised by disobedience to God. The world order is anti-God by nature; it is characterised by violent and obstinate disobedience to God and we naturally become like what we follow or worship.

4. **Whether Jews or Gentiles, what were the common forces *we* battled with and in turn what was *our* common fate (2:3)?** Although the Jews had been taught God's way and warned of the world order and Satan, they were no better off than the Gentiles because <u>both</u> were subjected to *the passions of our flesh, carrying out the desires of the body and the mind* (v3a). The *flesh* refers to both *body* and *mind*; we sin not only in our action but also in our thought. (The technical term for all going forth from our heart and will towards what God has forbidden is *concupiscence*.) For example, Jesus teaches: *everyone who looks at a woman with lustful intent has already committed adultery with her in his heart* (Matt. 5:28). Even the Jews who were under God's instruction could not escape the lure of the world and Satan because of *the flesh*; in their long history, they were disobedient to God, faithless to Him. Therefore there was no difference in our fate: we *were by nature children of wrath, like the rest of mankind* (v3b) – being

destined to face God's wrath is the universal human condition. Take a moment for this truth to sink in – it refutes the common belief that there are good people among us, the verses here state without ambiguity the reality of the human race. <u>Sin is endemic in our nature, and universal in its spread; no one is exempt. Sin is serious; it is the costliest thing in the whole of universe as judged by the eventual price paid to redeem us.</u>

The wages of sin is death (Rom. 6:23a). God's wrath is not a reality that we would like to face. Liberal Christians attempt to photoshop God's image and edit out His wrath, so we can dismiss it. Wrath is also commonly seen as incompatible with love: if God is loving, He cannot be wrathful, as the argument goes. But God's wrath is associated with God's attribute of holiness rather than love. Wrath is an expression of God's holiness towards everything that rebels against Him. When offended, if God had no reaction, His very nature of holiness would have been violated. It is incompatible for a holy God not to be hostile towards ungodliness and disobedience. Unlike our fit of rage, God's wrath is totally controlled, perfectly directed, absolutely just and completely holy. And rightly, we should be fearful because wrath is proportionate to God's holiness, which is perfect and excellent: *It is a fearful thing to fall into the hands of the living God* (Heb. 10:31). But love trumps it as His love towards us is also proportionate to His wrath towards us: *but God shows his love for us in that while we were still sinners, Christ died for us* (Rom. 5:8).

What are we saved from? From the wrath of the holy God and from the dominion of sin.

Application: In what sense have we already experienced God's wrath (Rom. 1:18-28)? Our society increasingly walks in darkness as its ideology and lifestyle move further and

Session 4: Ephesians 2:1-10

further away from the Bible. Hostility against God, the Bible and His people continues to intensify and proves the Bible right. People buy into Satan's deceptions which call evil good and good evil, and put darkness for light and light for darkness (Is 5:20). They also buy into Satan's biggest lie of all that there is no consequence to sin (Gen. 3:4). People take it as a licence to sin and sin to their hearts' content; scoffers tease, where is the promised judgement? They are emboldened when they think they can sin with impunity. But the very fact that they 'enjoy' their ungodly lifestyle and parade it with pride is a manifestation of God's wrath in the present age. Paul teaches in Romans 1 that God's wrath is first shown in God's giving them up to impurity, to dishonourable passions, to a debased mind, and to the unrestrained consequences of their actions. 'God gave them up' are chilling words, as for those given up only wrath remains.

How were we saved (2:4-9)

5. **What is the turning point in our fate (2:4)?** 'But God' is the phrase that signifies the turning point and gives us hope in the Bible. When we are at the end of the road, *but God* comes to our rescue! Thank God for the 'buts' in the Bible. We were spiritually dead in our trespasses and sins. We were not just seriously sick or nearly dead; we were dead and dead people could do nothing to save themselves. We need a rescuer, an external force to us, to save us. In our salvation, all initiatives lie with God. His mercy, His great love, is the first cause: *being rich in mercy, because of the great love with which he loved us* (v4). He also has *the immeasurable greatness of his power towards us who believe* (1:19) that He is able to *work all things according to the counsel of his will* (1:11). To make dead people come to life requires nothing less than the resurrection power He worked in raising Christ from the dead. God has both the goodness and power to will it.

6. **What are the three aspects of God's rescue work (2:5-6)?**
   <u>Spiritual death describes the separation of our soul from God.</u>
   <u>It follows that spiritual life is the union of our soul with God.</u>
   As sin has taken us captive and stands in the way, this union to make us alive can only be in Christ through His redemption work for us. *But God .... when we were dead in trespasses,* (i) <u>*made us alive* together with *Christ*</u> (v4, 5). We bring no merits to our salvation. It has been said that the only thing we contribute to our salvation is our sins! 'Nothing in my hand I bring, simply to the cross I cling.'[17] This is very humbling! Paul emphasises that it is *by grace we have been saved.*

To be set free from our sin, we need a double cure that breaks the chain of both its guilt and its power over us. Forgiveness is the cure for its guilt, but it is not enough for us to live a victorious life over sin. We need to be (ii) <u>*raised up with him*</u> (v6a), with the resurrection power living in us to resist sin. Before, we were dead in the trespasses; we could not resist sin. But now in Christ, sin has lost its grip on us. Although it is still present in our life, it does not have control over us and we in our new life have been given the power to resist sin. That is, it is our newfound freedom in Christ that we are able not to sin, compared to our previous state of being *un*able not to sin. In Christ, the dominion of sin over us has *already* brought to an end, so it is possible for us to resist sin even though it has *not yet* been destroyed in us.

We Christians live in the light of 'already' and 'not yet' of the gospel. In His death, resurrection and ascension, Christ has *already* done everything we need for salvation. But He has *not yet* brought His work to its consummation. [God] (iii) <u>*seated us with him*</u> in *the heavenly places in Christ Jesus* (v6). Note the

---

[17] From *Rock of Ages Cleft for Me*, by Augustus Toplady (1776).

Session 4: Ephesians 2:1-10

tense of the verb which emphasises the absoluteness of this promise as if it had already fully taken place. Once we are saved, we are moved out of the kingdom of darkness into the kingdom of light. Our new citizenship is in the kingdom of heaven even though we remain pilgrims in this present world. Christ enjoys the blessed immortality and glory, as represented by His sitting at the right hand in the heavenly places (1:20). Through our mystic union with Christ, what the head enjoys truly belongs to the members. Although we have *not yet* enjoyed the fullness of our inheritance, we have a sure pledge and foretaste in the person of Christ – we are *already* seated with Him in the heavenly places! We should be bursting with gratitude for these astonishing undeserved privileges that God lavishes on us beyond our wildest imagination!

Application: How does each aspect of God's rescue work affect our daily life? Passing from death to life is dramatic! With our newfound identity in Christ, we should, for example, begin to find a sense of fulfilment and purpose as God's intention for us (i.e. the union of our soul with God) is being lived out in our life. We should be more aware of the everlasting significance of how we live our life. Death and life are also the pattern how we combat sin still in our flesh. In Christ, we are united to Him in His death to sin and in His resurrection to new life. Bit by bit along our faith walk, we put to death the deeds of old self and put on our new self in our service to others. In this way, we make continuous progress in Christlikeness. <u>As we live for Christ and not for ourselves, our whole outlook of life is dramatically different. Faith lives out as our present reality the hope of our future glory in sharing Christ's triumph in the heavenly places.</u> With our royal identity secure, we have dignity that cannot be smashed, boldness to uphold godliness against the tides, and generosity towards others as a celebration of the riches that we have *already* abundantly received.

7. **What is the goal of God's rescue work (2:7)?** The design of God is to showcase His glory by these *immeasurable riches of his grace in kindness towards us in Christ Jesus* (v7), that His name will be lifted high, and praised with thanksgiving. Let's not forget that it is astonishing work of divine goodness that Gentiles are called into His kingdom as well as Jews. God's great kindness will be remembered *in the coming ages*. It means our duty that the great deeds of God shall be passed down to our children and our children's children. *We will not hide them from their children, but tell to the coming generation the glorious deeds of the LORD, and his might, and the wonders that he has done* (Ps 78:4).

Grace works (2:8-10)

8. **What is *this* that is *not our own doing*, but *the gift of God* in 2:8?** *This* definitely refers to something in the preceding phrase, namely, *by grace you have been saved through faith*. It means that *this* could refer to grace, our salvation or our faith. For Paul's additional comment that *this* is the gift of God not to be redundant, it is most likely to refer to *faith*, the immediate antecedent. If so, then, the verse is saying that by grace we are saved through faith. *This* faith though active in us is also the work of grace, the gift of God. It is not our own doing, i.e. not effected by our works, in order that no one would be able to boast ever! Although this faith is granted to us, we are actively engaged by doing the act of believing; God does not do the believing for us.

9. **Why is it important that *no one may boast* (2:9) about their salvation?** The ultimate goal of the salvation work is *to the praise of his glorious grace* (1:6) or *to the praise of his glory* (1:14).

Session 4: Ephesians 2:1-10

God is to have <u>all</u> the praise and enjoy the <u>maximum</u> glory. The purpose of our existence is to maximise His glory! In no way are we going to eclipse His glory. This is counter-intuitive to us because we by nature like to glorify ourselves, showing off our worth in what we have done rather than in what has been given us. In other words, we like to boast. In our flesh, we desire to be the sun, to be the source emitting brightness and the reason for praise. In Christ, however, we are like the moon, which emits no light on her own. The moon still shines but her glory is in reflecting the radiance of the sun. All that she can boast is the radiance of the sun. The more she boasts of Christ, the more glorious she is; there is no conflict. Maximum glory to God is for our maximum blessing (or felicity) because this is when we are most fulfilled! We who are in Christ are designed to be *vessels of mercy* (Rom 9: 23) to display the riches of God's glory.

Furthermore, we will come to realise that our salvation not being dependent on us is our greatest blessing. Just be honest with yourself, are we trustworthy in our ability, will and strength to sustain a perfect performance at all times? Do we ever falter in the face of trials? Have we ever had moments of weakness, doubt and hesitation? Do we always know what the right thing to do is in all situations? If our salvation is dependent on us in any way, however minutely it may be, we will be slave to that work, restless in our soul, and never sure of whether we have made it. So, for me, that *no one may boast* about his salvation is our Father knowing what is best for His children. <u>Assurance of faith</u> gives us peace, rest and joy that surpass all understanding as we sail through this life.

10. **In what ways are we God's *workmanship* and what is God's plan for us (2:10)?** From the Greek word for *workmanship* we get *poem*, a piece of literary workmanship. God works in those who belong to Him according to His will and for His

good pleasure. From God's hand it can only be masterpiece! What is this masterpiece that God is working in us? It is <u>our restoration</u>. We were made in God's image (Gen. 1:27), but since the Fall, it has been corrupted, severely marred beyond recognition. When we understand more about the seriousness of our sin and the extent of our corruption, one may wonder if it would have been easier to write us off and start afresh. But no, the covenant with Noah (Gen. 8:20-9:17) speaks of God's commitment to our restoration. Any restoration work is extensive, lengthy and painstaking. The goal is to let the glory of the original design of the Creator shine through again. Our very conservator-restorer is none other than our original Creator Himself. <u>Our restoration plan involves our redemption willed by the Father, accomplished by the Son and applied by the Spirit. Work is not finished at the point of our conversion; rather, it is only the beginning of the work to conform us to Christlikeness.</u> It is a lifelong process and will not reach its completion until we are on the other side of heaven. The process of putting off our old self and putting on our new self is extensive and comprehensive. Work is done at the deepest level of our being; it is most personal. It goes without saying that it can be painful and heart-rending. Yet all along, the Spirit is most tender and sensitive. <u>The pattern of death and resurrection, of deconstruction and reconstruction, or of pulling down and building up, is repeated in different issues and areas of our life and being.</u> Old wounds are opened up in order that they could be treated and heal. Sins are exposed till they are understood and combatted. In the process more of our old self dies so that more of the new self forms in us and we are worthy of our divine call. Fundamentally the good works of faith in our life is that *we should walk in them* (v10). This contrasts to our *walk* when we once were in darkness in verse 2. It is evidence of a genuine faith that we have a different *walk* from our past.

And I am sure of this, that he who began a good work in you will bring it to completion at the day of Jesus Christ (Phil. 1:6).
...work out your own salvation with fear and trembling, for it is God who works in you, both to will and to work for his good pleasure (Phil. 2:13).
Christ loved the church and gave himself up for her, that he might sanctify her, having cleansed her by the washing of water with the word, so that he might present the church to himself in splendour, without spot or wrinkle or any such thing, that she might be holy and without blemish (Eph. 5: 25-27). This is the beautifying work Christ has embarked on in every believer!

While we are not saved by good works, we are saved for *good works* (see Tit. 2:14, 2 Tim. 3:17). Moses was sent to deliver the Israelites from slavery in Egypt and God's request to Pharaoh was, 'Let my people go, that they may serve me' (Ex. 8:1). We are not saved to live whatever way we like, but to *good works* of God. Works that are done in man's own strength without faith cannot be good works in God's sight. *To the pure, all things are pure, but to the defiled and unbelieving, nothing is pure; but both their minds and their consciences are defiled. They profess to know God, but they deny him by their works. They are detestable, disobedient, unfit for any good work* (Tit. 1:15-16). *For whatever does not proceed from faith is sin* (Rom. 14:23).

These good works are not our own either but prepared by God for us to do beforehand (2:10). Yet elsewhere in the Bible says that we will be rewarded for them as if they were our merits. I find Spurgeon helpful in our understanding of this conundrum: 'God first works good works in us, and then He rewards us for them. This is a complex condescension and a mixed work of goodness.'[18] All is about Him and all glory to

---

[18] Spurgeon, Charles (1887) *Golden Alphabet*

Him; He is the greatest and most gracious towards us. We are honoured and humbled to be chosen and engaged in His grand plan for mankind.

Applications

11. Write a prayer of praise and thanksgiving in light of any new things you have learnt today or reminders that have caused your heart to leap for joy. Renew your commitment to God.

12. The unholy trio is the world, the devil and the flesh. How do you see the unholy trio is working in our society today?

Session 4: Ephesians 2:1-10

13. 'We little know how much of our virtue is due to our liberty. To be oppressed is to be tempted. Oppression drives men to wickedness' (Spurgeon, *Golden Alphabet*). Discuss its relevance to the temptations that Christians face today in our society.

14. Look back on the self-reflective questions at the start. What deeper understanding have you gained from this week's study on God's *workmanship* in you?

5. Divided No More [2:11-22]

Societies down the ages are plagued by division, hostility and prejudice, which are always present in the proud human heart. Division highlights differences, and it goes hand in hand with exclusivism. Social division could be done in a harsh and highly visible way of social segregation or done softly through society's tacit rules in people's behaviour. We may have a change in policy and/or law that pulls down the visible dividing wall but genuine acceptance is not automatic or guaranteed by a policy change. Our nature is such that we have a natural affinity to people who are similar to us with something in common. In contrast, differences give rise to suspicion, anxiety and dislike. It is also our nature that we like or love those whom we admire and aspire to be while we dislike those whom we loathe becoming ourselves. It means that while old divisions may be overcome, new ones will be forming as society evolves. Social cohesion seems to be an elusive ideal of our human attempts. In recent years, we see around the world the rise of 'identity politics' which might be called 'new tribalism' in politics.

Session 5: Ephesians 2:11-22

The opposite of division is unity, which is such a high human ideal that it is almost impossible to keep it long lasting. This is because human effort can only manage causes that unite for a time only and would soon shift. Therefore, the kind of unity that God's people strive for is truly out of this world. Jesus says that when unity is observed, the world will know where its source is and that we are His disciples. *The glory that you have given me I have given to them, that they may be one even as we are one, I in them and you in me, that they may become perfectly one, so that the world may know that you sent me and loved them even as you loved me* (John 17: 22-23).

In the context of human failure in achieving long-lasting unity among ourselves, we should be awestruck by the wonder of the gospel in dissolving deep-seated alienation present among man. The vision of God's will to unite (or 'sum up') all things in Christ (1:10) embodies the signature and beauty of the triune God. Standing in the way to this unity were three obstacles: the evil powers that had usurped dominion in this world, the spiritual deadness of the human race and the deep alienation among the people of the world. We see how God has moved towards His ultimate purpose by first enthroning Christ in the heavenly places (1:20) which is followed by making dead people alive together with their King (2:5). In today's study, we see how a new humanity has simultaneously arisen from Christ. This involves taking down the dividing wall of hostility (2:14). God has succeeded where we on our own effort have failed miserably because the unity forged by Him has a foundation out of this world. What we are gazing at in today's lesson is a vision of a miracle, which should arouse our sense of wonder and in turn our spontaneous praise of His glory.

Self-reflective questions

In your personal life, have you been confronted by a dividing wall or put up one yourself? In your experience, why is division more common than we desire? Why is it difficult to overcome?

The modern-day societies are increasingly polarised. What is the divisive issue of the day you are most concerned about? Can you see reconciliation of the two polar positions and why?

Remember our past (2:11-13)

1. **For all practical purposes, Ephesians chapters 1-3 are free of imperatives, while there are over forty imperatives in chapters 4-6. What is Paul's focus in the first half of the letter? Why is this important?** Paul's emphasis in the first three chapters of the letter is on understanding and communicating the gospel: what God has done and who He

is. Paul is jealous that believers know how richly blessed they are. This is not through asking for more but through knowing and understanding what are already in their possession that come with their identity in Christ. In other words, he is concerned about our spiritual growth in order that believers live fuller in Christ. Imperatives always flow out from indicatives. If we confuse the effects of the gospel with the gospel itself, what we believe and communicate will cease to be the gospel (good news) but moral teachings (a do-list).

2. **What is Paul's aim of asking the Gentiles to remember their past (2:11-12)?**
   - This is to strike home the contrast of before and after, and in turn to help us appreciate the glorious and gracious gospel that has been bestowed upon us. Paul is conscious that we understand as fully as we possibly can in order to know our God. A background of black velvet is to show off the sparkles of a diamond by contrast and makes us appreciate its glory and beauty all the more. This is to increase our joy and gratefulness because the state of being blessed but without our knowledge does not bring us happiness.
   - This is to remind us that there is no reason to be proud. In our sinful nature (Jews and Gentiles alike), we are prone to believe secretly that we somehow merit our salvation and all the blessings! Our past of hopelessness and helplessness reminds us that we are what we are today only because of grace.

3. **What was the long-standing hostility between Jews and Gentiles (2:11-17)?** God sovereignly chose the Jews to be His covenant people in the Old Testament, founding *the commonwealth of Israel* (v12) set apart from other nations. As such they were members of God's household while the Gentiles were *strangers and aliens* (v19). As His special people,

Jews were the recipient of His special blessing, protection and love. God also gave them strict and comprehensive laws governing all aspects of their life that they must live distinctly among nations and could not easily assimilate into another society. Another distinctive mark to set this special people apart was *circumcision* (v11); the law required all males to be circumcised on the eighth day after birth. Israel was supposed to be a great nation among all nations and the world would come to know the name of the Lord through their witness and revere Him. But Israel continually sinned. They perverted God's special favours and their distinction as a source of pride, isolation and vainglory. They observed the outward signs for their pride without heart. Their offerings were thus an abomination to the Lord. The fate of the nation was doomed as God judged the nation for their sins. By 586 BC, the kingdom was no more and people went into exile.

Jews treated Gentiles with contempt, calling them *the uncircumcision* as opposed to them *the circumcision* (v11). To counter their pride, Paul stressed that this mark was only external, *made in the flesh by hands* (v11), and did not certify a personal relationship with God. Jews saw Gentiles as 'unclean', so it was a common practice that a Jew would shake off the Gentile dust after entering Palestine in order not to contaminate the Holy Land. Alternatively they would go far out of their way in order to avoid entering the Gentile land altogether. Jonah was representative of their sentiment that most Jews did not want to share their great God with Gentiles. Instead, they desired to monopolise God and in turn keep their superior status which was the basis of their pride. This surely was not a people after God's own heart as God was clear that He would bring light to the Gentile nations (Isa. 42:6; 49:6; 60:3; 62:1-2).

Session 5: Ephesians 2:11-22

The hostility and hatred between the two groups was manifested in the harsh and visible dividing wall in the Temple that separated out the Court of the Gentiles. The sign on the dividing wall read, 'No Gentile may enter within the barricade which surrounds the sanctuary and enclosure. Anyone who is caught doing so will have himself to blame for his ensuing death.'[19]

Peter bore this disdain for Gentiles until God corrected him in a vision brought about by the gospel of Christ that *"What God has made clean, do not call common"* (Acts 10:15). He then was called to visit the household of Cornelius, a centurion. There he said to them, *"You yourself know how unlawful it is for a Jew to associate with or to visit anyone of another nation, but God has shown me that I should not call any person common or unclean"* (Acts 10:28). The gospel is revolutionary in breaking down social barriers that separate people. The long-standing acrimony between Jews and Gentiles ran so deep that its removal was unimaginable to them or to us. But Christ was able to provide the foundation for its overturn, and it was a radical change in people's attitude which could only be accomplished by the heavenly power.

4. **How does Paul describe who Gentiles once were (2:12-13)? Were Gentiles really *without* God (2:13)?** They were *separated from Christ, alienated from the commonwealth of Israel and strangers to the covenants of promise, having no hope and without God in the world.* As Christ is the foundation of hope and of all the promises, those *separated from Christ* have nothing but destruction. Gentiles were excluded not only from the outward signs, but also from everything necessary to the salvation and happiness of men. Therefore they were

---

[19] MacArthur, John, ibid., p. 77.

once *far off* from God and from salvation while the Jews *were near* (v17).

The problem with the Ephesians was not that they had no god but that they did not know the true God. They were not charged with atheism. After all the worship of Diana was prominent in the life of the city. Out of Christ there are none but idols, which are counted as nothing. According to Romans 1-2, God did not reject the Gentiles but the Gentiles rejected God, by suppressing the truth about God that He had made abundantly evident (Rom. 1:19-20).

One new man (2:13-18)

5. **How is Christ the linchpin in bringing forth *one new man in place of the two* (2:13-16, 18)?**
    - *For [Christ] himself is our peace* (v14), i.e. between Jews and Gentiles. Without Christ, enmity would have prevailed; there would have been no peace between God and men, so neither would there be peace among men. The just wrath of the holy God towards us because of our sins is propitiated by Christ. Consequently, Gentiles were once *far off* but now were *brought near* to God and salvation *by the blood of Christ*. Blood is the metonym for death. This is the language of the temple and its sacrifices.
    - Christ *has broken down in his flesh the dividing wall of hostility* (v14). The *blood* of Christ – the innocent One – paid the penalty for the sin of the guilty as the atoning sacrifice. The ceremonial law used to be the dividing wall between Jews and Gentiles, *but now* the death of Christ on the cross has fulfilled the symbolism of everything that took place in the temple and thereby brought about the abolition of *the law of commandments expressed in ordnances* (v15). In this way, Christ *has broken down in his flesh the dividing wall of hostility* (v14). *In his flesh* refers to Christ *being born in the*

Session 5: Ephesians 2:11-22

likeness of men (Phil. 2:7) and His death on the cross. The mark of difference, in circumcision, sacrifices, washings, abstaining from certain kinds of food and other laws, has been taken away because ceremonies as shadows of the realities have been abolished after the realities have arrived (Heb. 10:1). In His own body therefore has formed a perfect unity.

- Christ effected the reconciliation and has created *one new man in place of the two* (v15). Jews and Gentiles were not reconciled horizontally, for example, by a sudden change of heart in the Jews towards the Gentiles, or by Gentiles becoming proselytes and in turn more acceptable to the Jews. Instead, Christ is the *peace* (vv14 & 15) why we are united, that is, we are united to each other only because we are united to Jesus Christ. It is like in an orchestra, if each piece of instruments is tuned to the tuning fork of A, the orchestra will be automatically tuned to each other in unison. Christ has created a new humanity after the first Adam has failed, and it is a fellowship of grace. The first Adam sinned, and his sin led to curse, disintegration and death, a broken humanity. Christ as the second Adam came to undo all that. In Christ, Gentiles and Jews are equal. We are all sinners, needing the same thing, which is forgiveness of sins, offered in no other way than through the grace of Christ. There is no other way according to the gospel of Christ. Under His dominion is now a united people, realising the vision of God's will in 1:10. Jews have no choice but to admit Gentiles into fellowship with them or they won't have Christ as their Mediator or their peace! When Jews and Gentiles are reconciled to God, we are reconciled into *one body through the cross, thereby killing the hostility* (v16). In that body (i.e. the church) we see the *manifold*, or literally multi-coloured, wisdom of God (3:10).
- *For through him we both have access in one Spirit to the Father* (v18). We see in this verse the Trinity (Father, Son and the

Spirit) works in unison in our experience of peace and access. *Both* and *in one Spirit* stress the unity between Jews and Gentiles. We were *far off* and now we are brought *near*. It is made possible only *by the blood of Christ*. We do not possess access in our right; that right has to be granted to us. The Spirit who is in us testifies to the same truth, which is Christ, who is 'the door to the sheepfold' (John 10:1-14) that gives us the access to the Father. Our salvation is a trinitarian work: the Father willed it, the Son accomplished it and the Spirit applies it.

6. **Those who were far off refer to the Gentiles and** *those who were near* **refer to the Jews (v17). Who** *preached peace to you who were far off* **in v17? Was it Christ but how?** When Christ was still in the world, the gospel *peace* was not ready to be preached to the Gentiles. So, it was preached not by the lips of Christ but by the apostles after His ascension. The Gentiles were *far off* because they did not have the covenant promise of salvation. Their way to the kingdom of heaven made it necessary that Christ must rise from the dead, before the Gentiles can be called to the fellowship of grace. This was why Christ said to the Canaanite woman, *"Let the children be fed first, for it is not right to take the children's bread and throw it to the dogs."* (Mark 7:27). When Christ sent out the twelve, He also forbade them from going to the Gentiles: *Go nowhere among the Gentiles and enter no town of Samaritans, but go rather to the lost sheep of the house of Israel* (Matt. 10: 5-6). This geographical restriction was no longer valid after the departure of Christ. Now the command of believers is that *you will be my witnesses in Jerusalem and in all Judea and Samaria, and to the end of the earth* (Acts 1:6). However, in the sense that the preaching of the Word carries His authority, it can be said that *he preached peace to you who were far off* (v17), not by his own lips but through the apostles as His instruments. 'We need to recover this New Testament

teaching and learn to think of the preaching of the Word of God as an aspect of the ongoing work of Christ as Prophet.'[20] There is a difference between hearing Christ's voice through a preacher and hearing only the preacher's voice with his own wisdom in a sermon.

Whom we have become (2:19-22)

7. **Gentiles were once strangers and aliens to the covenants of promise. What is their status now (2:19-22)?** We are now *fellow citizens with the saints* and *members of the household of God*, living stones properly fitted into the building of the temple of the Lord (v22 cf. 1 Pet 2:5). This further reinforces the vision of a united people: if believers have no distinctions before God, they should have no distinctions among themselves. The conjunction *so then* reminds us that the basis of this change is what God – Father, Son and the Holy Spirit – has done for us. It also demonstrates the 'replacement rule' in Christian life: the passing of the old (whom we are no longer) and the coming of the new (whom we have become). This happens first in our status which takes place in a moment. The pattern however will repeat again and again as the gospel works its power through us to transform us into Christlikeness in our *inner being* (3:17).

8. **What is the structure of the holy temple of the Lord (2:20-21)?**

    - It is founded on the doctrine of *the apostles and the prophets* (v20), which centres on Christ. In this sense, Christ is actually the foundation on which the church is built by the preaching of doctrine. We know who the apostles were, but it is less clear as to who the prophets were. Calvin

---

[20] Ferguson, Sinclair, ibid., p. 67.

argued that they were the Old Testament prophets. The truth is that we cannot understand the New Testament without the Old Testament prophets! Their writings are in harmony with the apostles' because they have a common foundation (as Christ is the end of the law and the sum of the gospel). That is, they labour jointly in building the temple of God and it is one God who speaks in all of them. Our redemptive history is traced back to the creation of the world. The second interpretation is that the apostles and the prophets could be referred to the same people.

The third interpretation is to look at 4:11 where *the apostles and the prophets* are mentioned but in that context Paul distinguishes between them: 'the apostles appointed by the Lord (who, of course, were also prophets in their own right, bearers of divine revelation) and also others, (who were) prophets in the churches.'[21] John MacArthur expounds further: "[The New Testamen prophets] always spoke for God but did not always give a newly revealed message from God. The prophets were second to the apostles, and their message was to be judged by that of the apostles (1 Cor. 14:37). Another distinction between the two offices may have been that the apostolic message was more general and doctrinal, whereas that of the prophets was more personal and practical.'[22]

- *Christ Jesus himself [is] the cornerstone* (v20). It is difficult for us to understand the significance of the cornerstone in ancient buildings. Here is a description: 'the strength of buildings lies in their angles; and the cornerstone is that which unites and compacts the different sides of them; the chief cornerstone is that which is laid at the foundation,

---

[21] Ferguson, Sinclair, ibid., p. 71.
[22] MacArthur, John, ibid., p. 142.

Session 5: Ephesians 2:11-22

upon which the whole angle of the building rests, and which therefore is the principal support and tie of the whole edifice.'[23] Seeing this in the context of Jews and Gentiles as two separate walls which are formed into one spiritual building, it means that Christ is placed in the middle of the corner for the purpose of uniting both – so forceful is the metaphor!

- *In Christ, as the cornerstone, the whole structure, being joined together, grows into a holy temple in the Lord* (v21). Each believer is a unique living stone of the holy temple. It is true that each person, when viewed separately, is a temple where the Spirit dwells. But when joined to others, each person becomes a stone of the temple. This is a picture of unity of the church. The sanctification works of the Spirit in us *grow* us *in the Lord* and chisel us into our unique shapes to be properly fitted with one another. *In him you also are being built together into a dwelling place for God by the Spirit* (v22).

- When Solomon was building the temple, *it was with stone prepared at the quarry, so that neither hammer nor axe nor any tool of iron was heard in the house while it was being built"* (1 Kings 6:7). This life is where the quarry is for the living stones of God's holy temple. All the chiseling and moulding of us is done here, making us ready for heaven when we will slot in perfectly without further work. Does it give an extra dimension to our suffering now? Does this vision of purpose help us to endure it more joyfully? *Count it all joy, my brothers, when you meet trials of various kinds for you know that the testing of your faith produces steadfastness. And let steadfastness have its full effect, that you may be perfect and complete, lacking in nothing* (Jas. 1:2-4).

---

[23] Calvin's commentary on Ephesians, footnote 130, available online.

Applications

9. How has today's study given you a new vision for your church life and membership? What have you been inspired to do differently from now on?

10. Does your church mix well or are there distinct groups when comes to fellowship? How does your church foster integration of different groups?

Session 5: Ephesians 2:11-22

11. 'The Christian is called not to individualism but to membership in the mystical body.... That structural position in the Church which the humblest Christian occupies is eternal and even cosmic. The Church will outlive the universe; in it the individual person will outlive the universe. Everything that is joined to the immortal head will share His immortality... Personality is eternal and inviolable... It will not be attained by development from within outwards. It will come to us when we occupy those places in the structure of the eternal cosmos for which we are designed or invented.... We shall then first be true persons when we have suffered ourselves to be fitted into our places' (C. S. Lewis, *Membership*).

What have you been chasing in life to be your meaning? Have you ever seen the eternal significance of your church membership? How has God been chiselling you to make you fit properly into *the whole structure of the holy temple*?

6. Without Limits [3:1-21]

I wonder how the last study has left you and your group. From our experience, it is more common that we are divided than united. Some of the rifts we have in the world are long standing and hard to reconcile; others are emerging from new trends and polarise opinions. Unity that Paul speaks of is special because it is not forged by human hands but by Christ's atoning work on the cross and His resurrection. Believers are united only because we are united with Christ. Even as strangers to each other before, there exists now an unbreakable bond that we have in Christ. This unity is not one of uniformity. Rather, it celebrates our characteristics and differences by nurturing them to thrive in serving a united purpose in Christ. 'Unity in plurality' (St. Augustine's term) is God's unique design and in today's passage we will see it in *the manifold* (or multi-coloured) *wisdom of God* made known *through the church* (3:10).

In the last session, we see how we are being chiseled and moulded into our respective unique shapes to properly fit into God's grand scheme, taking our place as it were in the structure of the holy temple, into which the church is growing. Paul in

Session 6: Ephesians 3:1-21

today's passage tells us how God has fashioned him as the unique *living stone* to take his place assigned to him by God in the church. It was an epic story of an unlikely minister to the Gentiles! Let us not lose the sense of wonder when contemplating God's works. Rather, I believe it is Paul's desire to lift our heart to soar like an eagle beyond our imagination to reach the heavenly places and catch a glimpse of its glory. Then we will join in with Paul in praises to Him and be likewise frustrated by the limits of our language to capture the glory, the splendour and the majesty of the Infinite One.

Doxology is the goal of theology, as Paul demonstrates in the well-known verses of 3:20-21. St. Augustine expresses the difficulty of praising God in this way: 'Can any man say enough when he speaks of you? Yet woe betide those who are silent about you! For even those who are most gifted with speech cannot find words to describe you.'[24] Praising God is far from natural to us and our limitless God will challenge the limits of our minds and in turn our language. It is indeed an acquired and trained art, originated from our knowledge of Him, which we should be happy to engage in as it delights not only God but our own hearts too to glorify God and to enjoy Him for ever (Westminster Confession of Faith)!

Self-reflective questions

Do you find praising God natural to you? What are the difficulties you encounter?

---

[24] St. Augustine, *Confession*, translated by R. S. Pine-Coffin (1961), Penguin Classics, Bk1:Ch. 4.

The Making of Living Stones

How has studying Ephesians so far transformed you in the way you praise God? What have you learnt from Paul's teaching so far?

A prisoner for Christ Jesus (3:1-6)

1. **Chapter 3 begins with *For this reason*. For what reason does Paul refer to (3:1, see also 3:6)?** Paul is referring to what he has been expounding in 2:11-22, the great mystery that a new man has been created in place of the two in Christ, ending the age-old hostility between Jews and Gentiles by tearing down the dividing wall of the Mosaic law in its fulfilment in Christ. And now who are the Gentiles if they accept the gospel? Paul sums it up succinctly in verse 6: *The mystery is that the Gentiles are fellow heirs, members of the same body, and partakers of the promise in Christ Jesus through the gospel.* The believing Gentiles are admitted into the God's household and their *togetherness* with the Jews is stressed. After this mystery had been revealed, someone must be sent to bring the gospel to the Gentiles. More specifically, Paul was the apostle of the Gentiles (1 Tim. 2:7). *For this reason*, his whole life was changed; this was how knowing the mystery had affected him. The fact that he, a Jew, brought the gospel to the Gentiles was a testimony of this mystery.

Session 6: Ephesians 3:1-21

2. **How does Paul understand his imprisonment (3:1-2)?** Paul was imprisoned by the Roman authority, but he did not consider himself a prisoner of Rome. Rather, in his perspective, he was *a prisoner for Christ Jesus on behalf of you Gentiles* (v1). It shows how Christ-centred in Paul's thinking. His imprisonment was for Christ's saving purpose to the Gentiles. His chains served to prove and declare his calling. He expressed no regrets or shame about his chains but a sense of honour to be useful to Christ in bringing the gospel to the Gentiles and as such serving as a pivotal vehicle in the unfolding of the great mystery to the world. For that, if the chains could not be avoided, he was willing.

The phrase *'assuming you have heard'* does not necessarily suggest that Paul was addressing people who did not know him but that his readers had indeed heard of him. It is also perfectly plausible that among them there were new members after Paul had left and he trusted that the church had remained faithful to his teaching. As the apostle for the Gentiles, Paul was given *the stewardship of God's grace* (i.e. the gospel) *for you*, the Gentiles (v2).

3. **How did Paul know he was sent to the Gentiles (3:3-6)? Why did his readers need to be made aware of it? How did he propagate the message?** The mystery of oneness between Jews and Gentiles in Christ was revealed to him and those who read what he had written about it would see that he had *[his] insight into the mystery of Christ* (v4), which was a special work of God. So how did Paul come to know Christ? First it was *revelation* and then he experienced ongoing *illumination* into the revelation, which combined to give the fullness of his understanding of the gospel. The gospel preached by Paul is not a human creation. This mystery was not known before by anyone in other generations but *has now been revealed to his holy apostles and prophets by the Spirit* (v5). The calling of the

Gentiles was a truly revolutionary idea given the cultural background of the time and the long-standing hostility between the two groups; no one could have dreamt up the vision and with such extensive scope. The New Testament saints have much better sight than the Old Testament saints because Christ has come and He was the fulfilment of all Old Testament promises. Now the Gentiles have the same status as the Jews (*fellow heirs, members of the same body*) and stand to inherit *the same promise in Christ Jesus through the gospel* (v6). We are all in on this secret! Paul propagated it not only by *proclamation* but also by *inscripturation* (v3) that even *we* get to read about it in the Scriptures and know.

An unlikely minister in Paul (3:7-13)

4. **What was the power behind Paul's transformation (3:7-9)? Why did he labour on the point that he was 'less than the least of all the saints' (3:8)?** Paul wants to stress that it is grace from start to finish with no contribution from him except his unworthiness, so all *to the praise of his glorious grace* (1:6). He was made a steward of grace to others but he himself was totally dependent on grace. The choice was not his at all. It was not his education, natural abilities, power, influence, personality or any other credentials that had qualified him for the position; if anything, his personal factors should have disqualified him, not least being a fervent persecutor of the church and therefore his Master before his conversion. The choice was *the gift of God's grace* (v7). *Grace was given* (v8) to him in order that he preached grace to the Gentiles (v9). <u>The gospel and its ministry flow out from grace and point to grace.</u> An important lesson to ministers is that they live out of the same resources to which their ministry is pointing people to.

Before he was made a minister of Christ by God's grace, he was an ardent and zealous persecutor of His church. On a

Session 6: Ephesians 3:1-21

mission to further hunt down Christians, he was converted on the road to Damascus. When being sent to Paul, Ananias, a disciple at Damascus, had this verdict about him: *Lord, I have heard from many about this man, how much evil he has done to your saints at Jerusalem. And here he has authority from the chief priests to bind all who call on your name* (Acts 9:13-14). Because of this reputation, Paul had a hard time initially to be accepted into the church: *they were all afraid of him, for they did not believe that he was a disciple* (Acts 9: 26). So, when he described himself as 'less than the least of all the saints' (v8), this was not feigned humility but his honest opinion of himself that he was the most unlikely person to be made a minister of Christ. As he highlights his unworthiness, God's grace is all the more exalted as the power behind first his own calling and then the fruitfulness of his ministry. To make something great out of nothing shows the effectual working of His power.

5. **From the example of Paul, what do we see as the pattern of God's calling to individual (1 Cor. 1:27-31, see also Session 5 Q8)?** For one who experiences so deeply God's grace working in his own personal life, Paul is well placed in preaching with conviction to the Gentiles *the unsearchable riches of Christ, and to bring to light for everyone what is the plan of the mystery hidden for ages in God who created all things* (v9). *The riches of the Messiah* to the Gentiles who were once without hope and without God in the world? This idea is mindboggling. The choice of Paul, among all people, to be entrusted with this groundbreaking task and privilege of revealing this hidden mystery to the world also raises eyebrows in terms of his suitability. But God has His *wisdom* in His way, which defies our human expectations. This is why His way is often offensive to our natural mind. Yet there is a deep appropriateness of God's choice. Paul is not only a minister but also himself a powerful witness of what he

preaches. His incredible transformation, from being a relentless enemy to a zealous apostle of the gospel, is an embodiment of the gospel power, making him fit for God's special use of him. We as living stones of God's holy temple are more like unique jigsaw pieces than stones of uniform shape and dimensions (see Session 5 Q8). 'This pattern in which the context and experience of calling and the specific burden of an individual are integrally related is not unusual. Think, for example, of Isaiah (Isa. 6:1ff) and Jeremiah (Jer. 1:1ff). The burden of their ministries was an expression of the way in which God had called them to serve him. It is often this way and was so for Saul of Tarus.'[25]

6. **What is the eternal purpose of God through the church and how is it realised (3:10-12)?** God's eternal purpose for the fullness of time is to unite all things in Christ, things in heaven and things in earth (1:10) and give glory to Himself (1:12). 'Heaven and earth' means the whole of creation, spiritual and material. This requires *the immeasurable greatness of his power towards us who believe* (1:19) to bring it to fruition. We have been studying how extraordinary it is that God's people are united into a new humanity in Christ, called the church, through which *manifold wisdom of God* is manifested (v10).

The *wisdom of God* is embodied in everything He does and bears His own character. He has the power to bring to pass all that He wills. His way and deeds are higher than ours, are the best and perfect. It lacks nothing and it cannot be improved by any addition or subtraction. *I perceived that whatever God does endures for ever; nothing can be added to it, nor anything taken from it* (Ecc. 3:14a).

---

[25] Ferguson, Sinclair (2005), ibid., p. 81.

Session 6: Ephesians 3:1-21

In the context of verse 10, the *wisdom of God* refers specifically to that displayed in the life and existence of the church, i.e. God's salvation plan for us. In His incarnation, crucifixion and resurrection, Christ gave birth to the church. He is the cornerstone that unites the separate walls of Jews and Gentiles. This wisdom displayed through the church is *manifold* or, literally, *multicoloured* as in Jacob's *robe of many colours* to Joseph (Gen. 37:3). Through the church unity in plurality is displayed a new humanity whereby people in rich diversity are worked by the Spirit to fit together in the body.

This display of God's wisdom in relation to the church is especially to enlighten *the rulers and authorities in the heavenly places* (v10) who are the holy angels. The mystery was hidden from them too but being in the same household of God, Peter tells us that they long to look into the matters of the church (1 Pet 1:12). In the fullness of time, the church will be united with them also, forming God's household.

This eternal purpose is *realised in Christ Jesus our Lord*. In Him, God will be triumphant in fulfilling His plan and our victory is sure. Therefore, *we have boldness and access with confidence through our faith in him* (v12).

7. **How does Paul encourage his readers concerning his imprisonment (3:13)?** It is easy to lose heart and feel dejected when 'bad' fortune strikes. It may also cause doubt on the cause if you see your leader suffer. But Paul encourages the Ephesians to gain a divine perspective in digesting his affliction. <u>Suffering is the path to glory</u>; it is for his glory but also for their glory (and ours!). We know how affliction refines us individually and draws us near to Christ as we partake in His suffering. But with Paul, his suffering works to advance the gospel, and he has the final glorification of the Ephesians in mind as they are now brought in to be part of

God's household. So, he asks the Ephesians *not to lose heart* for <u>God is still working out His divine plan for them even in his weakness</u>.

The prayer (3:14-21)

8. **This section is again opened with *For this reason*. For what reason does Paul refer to in 3:14 (cf. 3:1)?** The reason for the prayer that follows is to be found in the preceding verses 1-13. To the extent that verses 1-13 refers to its preceding verses in 2:11-22, the prayer in this section is a response to the now revealed mystery of oneness in Christ independent of ethnicity and other earthly distinctions. But between verse 1 and verse 14, Paul has added his personal dimension. He shows his conviction of this truth by willingly pouring himself out as a drink offering for this mission to the Gentiles. Paul's love for the Ephesians mirrors Christ's love for us. While God alone acts upon us, He acts by His own instruments. In reaching out to the Gentiles, Paul's faith was instrumental in ushering in this new era, at the expense of his own comfort or safety. To encourage his readers, Paul leads them into prayer for their understanding of their resources as one in Christ. This prayer flows out from the first one of 1:15ff. Paul prays that like his, believers' life would be impacted by the knowledge of Christ, *strengthened* (v16) and *filled* (v19).

9. **What does 'bowing the knees' represent (3:14)?** This is not a prescribed posture for prayer. Rather, 'bowing the knees' is an expression of reverence commonly employed. It evokes the prophecy of Isaiah: *'To me every knee shall bow, every tongue shall swear allegiance'* (Isa. 45:23). It is of significance that this worship to the exalted God comes after an invitation issued *to the ends of the earth* to turn to the Lord and be saved (Isa. 45: 22). This is fulfilled in Christ, *so that at the name of Jesus every*

Session 6: Ephesians 3:1-21

knee should bow, in heaven and on earth and under the earth, and every tongue confess that Jesus Christ is Lord, to the glory of God the Father (Phil. 2:10). As Paul is contemplating the works of Christ and what He has accomplished, he does not wait till the last day but to give Him the worship and honour that is due to His name now.

10. **To which family do believers belong now (3:15), compared with who they once were?** We now belong to God's household, which are one family and one race through Christ. And this household includes angels too. All things will be united in Christ, things in heaven and things on earth (1:10). Previously the Ephesians were united in the worship of Goddess Diana. They must have contributed one way or another to the building of the gigantic temple dedicated to her. Strictly speaking, they were her family, over which she presided as the common mother and patroness. Now Paul told the believers in Ephesus that in contrast, they belonged to a nobler family, with God as their common Father, *from whom every family in heaven and on earth is named* (v15).

11. **What is this prayer essentially about and how does *strengthening* take place (3:16-17)?** Essentially the prayer is about <u>spiritual growth</u>. If knowledge does not bring renewal of the mind and transformed life, it is not really believed. Day by day we grow stronger and advance in our spiritual stature. Calvin says it well: 'believers have never advanced so far as not to need farther growth. The highest perfection of the godly in this life is an earnest desire to make progress.' However, we cannot rely on our own effort or ability to actualise this progress. Instead, 'it is a gift of the grace of God, not only that we have begun to run well, but that we advance; not only that we have been born again, but that we

grow from day to day.' [26] That is, <u>both our salvation and our subsequent spiritual growth are the fruit of grace</u>. First, this *strengthening* is *granted* to us *according to the riches of his glory*. That is, it is a gift of God and Paul testifies that he has personally tasted it (vv1-13). Secondly, this *strengthening* is the work and power of the *Spirit*, and not of our own. Thirdly, this work is directed to the *inner being* as opposed to the outward man. Fundamentally, spiritual progress advances outward from *inner being* or the soul. Paul further identifies those whom God gifts spiritual vigour are those in whom *Christ dwells* (v17) and the method is *through faith* (v17). <u>Faith therefore is not an intellectual concept; it brings Christ near that we are convicted of the truth about Him and feel His warmth</u>. Paul also specifies the place where He dwells in us – i.e. *in our hearts*. It is not enough to house knowledge in the head or let it sit on our lips. It has to be in the heart to make a difference in our life.

12. **What is the end of this strength (3:18-19) and what is the enabling power (3:17b)?** The end of the *strengthening* is to comprehend fully the love of Christ, which is, ironically, so vast and deep that it is beyond our comprehension. Our starting point is our experiential knowledge of it in our life; *being rooted and grounded in love* (v17), we have a taste of the power and the character of Christ's love working in our personal life. This is the basis for us to recognise Christ's love in others, so *with all the saints*, past and present and future collectively, we *may have the strength to comprehend ... what is the breadth and length and height and depth* (v18). The four dimensions represent the complete perfection of this wisdom. No man can approach God without being raised above himself and above the world: *that [we] may know the love of*

---

[26] Calvin's commentary on Ephesians,, available online.

Session 6: Ephesians 3:1-21

Christ that surpasses knowledge (v19). The impact of gaining such a sight on us is to *be filled with all the fullness of God*; he who has Christ has everything necessary to be made perfect in God.

We are not aware of our limits until we are shown something bigger! If we are not aware of our limits, our limits will work to limit us by limiting our God! Once we have gone over the surpassing-our-knowledge zone, we see God as without limits! God has proven it when Paul shows us the lengths He has got into to accomplish 'the mystery of Christ' which is beyond what we can ask and think. We see better who God is and begin to be *filled with all His fullness*; we have broken free from our limits.

Application: How do you picture the breadth, length, height and depth of Christ's love?

Doxology – the goal of theology! (3:20-21)

13. **Ephesians 3:20-21 is a well-known benediction with which to close a worship service. Having studied its context, what new insights have you gained in it?** This doxology concludes the first half of this letter where Paul works hard to raise our eyes towards the lofty things of God, the mystery that the angels long to see. There is a sense that he cannot

adequately express in words the reality he points us to. He labours to build up our vision beyond ourselves in order to contemplate God's plan in the cosmic scale! 'In the classroom of God's universe, He is the Teacher, the angels are the students, the church is the illustration, and the subject is the *manifold wisdom of God* (3:10).'[27] <u>The church is the illustration of God's divine purpose of all things!</u> His deeds speak of His power, goodness, perfection and wisdom. Having better grasped the greatness of His past deeds, which has surpassed all our imagination, can we doubt His commitment to bringing His Word to pass in the fullness of time? Is it even possible for Him to withhold anything from us fulfilling His purpose?

From His deeds already done, we should have the unswerving confidence that our Lord *is able to do far more abundantly than all that we ask or think, according to the power at work within us* (v20). His goodness and wisdom are not going to be limited by our ability to ask or indeed, our inability to conceive what we might ask! <u>There is no limit to what God can achieve for His people.</u> But *he gives more grace* (Jas 4:6) than whatever our needs are! We should not fear asking Him for too many or bold blessings, as long as they are in accordance with His will. This is our God. This leaves us nothing else to say except to praise His name: *to him be glory in the church and in Christ Jesus throughout all generations, for ever and ever. Amen.*

We see God's glory in the visible expression of His invisible perfection, a display of His personal characteristics. Paul is praying that the fellowship of the church will display none other than what uniquely of God, i.e. His glory! His glory is also being displayed in Christ Jesus. *For all the promises of God*

---

[27] MacArthur, John, ibid., p.97.

Session 6: Ephesians 3:1-21

find their Yes in him. That is why it is through him that we utter our Amen to God for his glory (2 Cor 1:20). 'Amen is the word of positive response, confirmation, and affirmation used in the Old Testament. Its Hebrew root means to be faithful, reliable, true… Jesus himself is the true Amen (Rev 3:14).'[28]

Applications

14. 'Believers have never advanced so far as not to need farther growth. The highest perfection of the godly in this life is an earnest desire to make progress' (Calvin, see also Q11). Are you earnestly seeking for your spiritual growth? What do you discern about God's will for you in your spiritual training?

15. Life changes with conviction of the gospel truth; Paul became the unlikely minister of the gospel to the Gentiles. How has your conviction of the gospel truth changed your life?

---

[28] Ferguson, Sinclair (2005), ibid., p. 97.

16. What encouragements do you find in 3:20-21? People's attention often falls on verse 20 rather than verse 21. What does it show about our hearts?

Our position or our viewpoint often suggests helplessness, which means we have reached the end of our limits. But with this doxology, we are never hopeless because God is not bound by our limits. Instead, *he is able to do far more than we ask or think.* He is our mighty Helper! This is no wishful thinking because we know that *power at work within us* and in history – the deposit of the Holy Spirit has testified to us.

It is popular to have verse 20 as our favourite verse. Who wouldn't? We feel good to be so empowered especially at times of distress. We have our encouragement and find our comfort; we feel energized to keep going. Our religion often stops at ourselves, our immediate concerns and this life. The focus is very much on ourselves. However, verse 21 reminds us that the end of our religion is not ourselves but Christ. Many of us love verse 20 for ourselves and pay lip service to verse 21: *to him be glory in the church and in Christ Jesus throughout all generations, for ever and ever. Amen.* We must not forget everything is to His glory and for His glory – He is the object of our worship and praising Him is what we are created to do! We exist to show Him off as great and excellent and not the other way. Jesus healed ten lepers but only one turned back to praise Him with a loud voice (Luke 17:11-19). May we not be one of the nine lepers who receive grace and are concerned of our own benefits but do not praise Him for who He is.

Session 6: Ephesians 3:1-21

17. The doxology of 3:20-21 'represents a build up of thought that breaks through the limits of language' (Ferguson, *Let's study Ephesians*, p. 95). Now write a prayer praising God, pushing the limits of your language to reflect your deepened understanding of His love.

7. Becoming Worthy [4:1-16]

Ephesians is a letter of two halves, which are linked by the conjunction 'therefore' (4:1).[29] Therefore, it is clear in Paul's mind that the first half is the basis, or the reason, or the cause, for the second half. Reading the two halves without one another will not be complete. The first half is devoted to communicating the gospel truth and understanding God's will. It grounds believers' understanding of their identity firmly in God's cosmic plan stretching from eternity past to eternity future! For all practical purposes, the first half is an imperative-free zone. Instead, it engages us, as far as our minds could be stretched, to grasp all the fullness of God, from which all blessings flow! The Truth about our identity in Christ is forceful and makes demands on us if we are honest with its implications. Paul works out its practical response in the second half, characterised by dozens of imperatives which flow out swiftly and naturally from the gospel truth expounded in the first half.

Therefore, reading the first half without the second would

---

[29] The word 'therefore' appears in ESV, NKJV and NASB but not in NIV.

Session 7: Ephesians 4:1-16

keep the knowledge of God academic and miss the essence of Christian life, which is renewal and transformation. Reading the second half without the first would turn Christian life into self-improvement with a set of moral teachings cut off from the gospel power. <u>We have legalism when God's commands are divorced from His person.</u> As we start delving into the second half of the letter, let us remember from the first half the God of grace as its propelling force.

Self-reflective questions

In what ways is church life crucial to your faith walk?

Which aspect(s) of church life do you find most difficult?

Be worthy (4:1)

1. **The second half can be summed up in one exhortation given in 4:1. What is it? What may be believers' reservation in thinking that they are 'worthy' (cf. 2:8-9)?** Paul urges us *to walk in a manner worthy of the calling to which we have been called* (v1), which is the summary of the second half of the letter. In the following three chapters, he lays out in detail what this one exhortation looks like in all aspects of our lifestyle. At first glance, this seems to be at odds with the teaching that has gone before, which says that our salvation is God's grace from start to finish and no one may boast except in our Lord Jesus Christ. In his own testimony also, Paul highlights his own <u>unworthiness</u> and exalts the grace of God. He himself lives out of the very same resources to which his ministry points; that is, the minister and those being ministered are no difference but the work of God's grace. So, what is this call to us of 'being worthy of the gospel'?

The Greek word for *worthy* is *axios* which has the root meaning of balancing the scales. It means that one side is expected to come up to the corresponding weight on the other side. Therefore, rather than suggesting that we somehow merit the grace of God, the calling of being *worthy* here is to live a life that is 'fitting' or 'appropriate' to match our corresponding high status (i.e. *the calling*) as adopted sons in God's royal household and fellow heirs with Jesus Christ – familiarity can be our enemy in comprehending that this is a high status and therefore a high calling! <u>To be *worthy* is a call that our practical living matches our spiritual position</u>; in other words, we grow into the substance of who we now are in Christ. At the beginning we cannot fully comprehend the extent God has blessed us (see the cascade of blessings in 1:3-14) due to the narrowness and weakness of our minds. But as we grow in our knowledge of God, as Paul earnestly prays

Session 7: Ephesians 4:1-16

that we do (1:17-23), the weightiness of *the calling to which we have been called* will slowly dawn on us and in turn our practical living would have to match up in our *worthiness* in Christ.

The Old Testament notes this character of God concerning scales: *A just balance and scales are the LORD's; all the weights in the bag are his work* (Prov. 16:11) and *Unequal weights and unequal measures are both alike an abomination to the LORD* (Prov. 20:10). Included in God's writing on the wall to announce His judgement on the Babylonian king Belshazzar was *TEKEL, you have been weighed in the balances and found wanting* (Dan. 5:27). God expects our obedience following our salvation by grace; it is non-negotiable. *Walk* refers to our daily conduct, day-to-day living. In contrast with our previous *walk* in 2:1-10, we now have a new *walk* in Christ. The work of the Spirit in our *inner being* (3:16) will naturally manifest in our *walk*. <u>Becoming *worthy of the calling* simply means becoming more like the Lord Jesus.</u>

2. **Why does Paul make this appeal as *a prisoner of the Lord* (4:1)?** He is talking as someone who has the first-hand experience of all that he is commanding us to do:
   - He reminds us how his whole life has been changed by the gospel and for the gospel;
   - He is not ignorant of how costly this worthy Christian walk can be;
   - Despite that, his commitment is total; and
   - His readers are reminded the high personal cost for him to bring them the gospel, so he has at least earned our attention for what he has to say on the impact it should make to us individually and corporately.

The church family (4:2-6)

3. **The first noticeable change to our life is the new family we have gained! What is the basis of this church family (4:2-6 cf. Matt. 12:46-50)? What is the one word that Paul keeps repeating in 4:4-6?** *And stretching out his hand towards his disciples, he said, "Here are my mother and my brothers! For whoever does the will of my Father in heaven is my brother and sister and mother"* (Matt. 12:49-50). *For he who sanctifies and those who are sanctified all have one source. That is why he is not ashamed to call them brothers* (Heb. 2: 11).

In Christ, we have gained a new family, and according to Christ, this bond is stronger even than our blood ties. Paul has been expounding the mystery of Christ that unites Jews and Gentiles *in the bond of peace* (v3). Who were previously strangers to each other, enemies even, are now united as one in Christ and become brothers and sisters to one another. What does this family look like? How are we supposed to relate to one another? This was an unchartered territory to the first-century believers. Paul here spells it out.

Verse 3 suggests that church family is defined by *the unity of the Spirit in the bond of peace* already exists because Paul says our relationship with one another is to *maintain* or *preserve* this unity, not to create or forge it anew. In the subsequent three verses, Paul uses the word *one* seven times! This unity is on a seven-fold foundation, with verse 4 centring on the Spirit, verse 5 on the Son and verse 6 on the Father. Christ is one body what has many parts. In it, there are no more earthly distinctions, such as Jews or Gentiles, males or females, slaves or freemen, and so on. The church now shoulders the important mission to make visible the invisible God, i.e. to glorify Him. All parts of the body are united in this same purpose. The same Spirit dwells in each one of us,

Session 7: Ephesians 4:1-16

which gives us the deepest common reality that the Spirit makes our lives home for the Father and the Son (cf. John 14:23). The Spirit also testifies to us that the one hope we all share in our calling (1:11-14) is true.

We are united in *one Lord* – our saviour Jesus Christ. *One faith* refers not to our personal faith but to the body of doctrine revealed in the New Testament; all truths of the Bible converge to this one Truth about the one Lord Jesus Christ. We all share the same sign (*one baptism*) of our belief, our identity in Christ and union with Him (Rom. 6:1-11).

Each of us confesses the *one God*. That 'the Lord is our God, the Lord is one' is the basic doctrine of Judaism. We all have the same *Father* with our adoption. He is *over all* (sovereign), *through all* (omnipotent) and *in all* (omnipresent). It is a glorious and comprehensive statement about our God that 'We are God created, God loved, God saved, God Fathered, God controlled, God sustained, God filled, and God blessed.'[30]

The profound spiritual oneness that underpins the physical oneness of our church family is something new and unsurpassable by any other human relationship.

4. **What are the virtues of Christians 'walking worthily' in the Lord that help *maintain* this unity in the fellowship (4:2-3)?**

- *Humility* is the first step to unity and every Christian virtue has its roots in it. The root meaning of the Greek word for *humility* is 'lowly-mindedness'. It is not a false demeaning of ourselves. <u>The only source of true humility is a proper understanding of the doctrines of grace;</u>

---

[30] MacArthur, John, ibid., p.131.

nothing we have except what we have received by grace. A proper view of God and proper self-awareness of our unworthiness are two sides of the same coin. We will see genuine humility expressed when one moves out of a self-centred orientation and into a Christ-centred orientation in life. It is interesting to note that the Greek word for *humility* was coined by Christians, probably by Paul himself, as 'neither the Romans nor the Greeks had a word for humility.' [31] It was 'unnatural' for anyone not to think of himself with pride and self-satisfaction. To the pagans, humility was a pitiable weakness. This worthy Christian walk is truly revolutionary to our nature!

- *Gentleness* or *meekness* is one of the surest signs of true humility. It is often associated with timidity and weakness, which is far from the biblical meaning. Gentleness describes someone who is mild-spirited, self-controlled and not vengeful. The Greek word for *meekness* 'was used of wild animals that were tamed, especially of horses that were broken and trained. Such an animal still has his strength and spirit, but its will is under the control of its master.... Meekness is power under control. Biblical meekness, or gentleness is power under the control of God.'[32] <u>To be meek is to forget ourselves altogether and have God as everything.</u>

- *Patience* means long-suffering or long-tempered. It is a virtue to endure without giving up. Patience takes a long-term view and produces *forbearance to one another in love*, acknowledging that we are all 'works-in-progress' and how our Lord has been patient with ourselves.

---

[31] MacArthur, John, ibid., p.120, quoting John Wesley.
[32] MacArthur, John, ibid., p.124-5.

Session 7: Ephesians 4:1-16

- The above Christian virtues will serve to *eager[ly] maintain the unity of the Spirit in the bond of peace* (v3). This unity cannot be created by organisation. Rather, it is the work of the Holy Spirit in every believer. It comes from inside, not outside. <u>It is not organisational but spiritual unity of true believers</u>, whose eagerness in maintaining the unity comes from the unstoppable outworking of the gospel in their lives. <u>Taking the Christian virtues together, this unity is sustained not by self-promotion but by self-denial.</u>

The Church is His triumph (4:7-11)

5. **Verse 7 starts with the conjunction 'but'. How does 4:7 qualify the 'oneness' of the church in 4:4-6?** Unity that is forged by humans often presses uniformity on people. But God's trademark in His design is unity in plurality, His *manifold wisdom* (3:10), which to us seems to be a baffling paradox and yet with unspeakable beauty. This explains the conjunction 'but' to start verse 7 to contrast <u>the unity of the church with the rich diversity in grace and gifts God blesses each of the believers with.</u> The emphasis is on *each one of us*. We are made unique, endowed with *grace given to each one of us according to the measure of Christ's gift*. This grace-gift from Christ is specially tailored and measured out in exact proportion to each one of us. We are to function in different ways to make this church body work. <u>Unity is fostered by us using our unique gifts and graces to complement each other, all serving the same purpose.</u> As we are unique, we are <u>irreplaceable,</u> as opposed to interchangeable, members of the church body. Like in a family, a member gone leaves an empty chair. <u>There are no redundant members either;</u> if any member does not pull his weight (not working his gifts for the glory of God), the church suffers as a whole. While no gifts should be unused, no gifts should be exalted either.

Here the virtue of true humility (as discussed above) functions to maintain unity.

What is grace? The usual definition is being given what is unmerited, unearned and undeserved. God's nature is to give; as He is self-sufficient, He needs nothing from us. Reflecting this nature, grace is much more about giving than getting. And the greatest gift of grace is self. God gives us not only blessings but also above all Himself! Grace is initiated by God and we have nothing to do with it. God has the sovereign choice over what, how and how much to gift to us, according to His plan, purpose and measure. 'God is the source of electing grace, equipping grace and enabling grace.' Enabling grace ensures that our labour with our special gifts is not in vain but function to the glory of God. 'When the Holy Spirit gave us our gift, He presented us with precisely the right blend of abilities and enablement we need to serve God. Not only does our unique giftedness make us an irreplaceable member of Christ's body but it is a mark of God's great love to single each of us out for unique blessing and ministry.'[33] *All these are empowered by one and the same Spirit, who apportions to each one individually as he wills* (1 Cor. 12:11). The corollary is that we should not envy what God has assigned others to do but be content and focused on what God has assigned to us specifically to do.

6. **Verse 8 evokes Psalm 68:18. How did Christ win the right to distribute gifts to His people (4:8-10)?** Verse 8 evokes Psalm 68:18 which is a song of triumph. In the ancient world, the triumphal procession went through the capital city with a long line of captives from war, and chariots and horses carrying the booty of his victory. These were jubilating occasions overflowing with public acclaim and lavish display

---

[33] MacArthur, John, ibid., p.137.

Session 7: Ephesians 4:1-16

of gratitude. When God's people were being oppressed, it was easy to imagine that God was somehow idle and asleep. But when He suddenly stretched out His arms of deliverance, it was as if He roused Himself and *ascended on high* to take His throne of judgement. We see God's magnificence when He roars and acts against His enemy!

Paul sees its fulfilment in the noblest triumph of Christ when He, subduing sin, conquering death, defeating Satan and all power of hell, rose majestically to heaven, that He might exercise His glorious reign over the Church. Rather than parading prisoners-of-war, Christ's campaign was to set the captives of the enemy free (Isa. 61:1) and return them to whom they belong! No ascension is more glorious than Christ's to the right hand of the Father after His death and resurrection. From the heavenly places He might rule over all authorities and powers, and become the everlasting protector and guardian of the Church. Instead of *receiving gifts among men* as in Psalm 68:18, Paul's citation says *he gave gifts to men* (v8). What is the intention of *receiving gifts* if it is not to *give gifts*? <u>After Christ's ascension came all the gifts empowered by the Holy Spirit (John 7:39, 14:12; Acts 2:33). The victorious King distributes the spoils to the members of His Church. This was how He has won His right to give gifts to His people.</u>

Paul is quick to reason in verse 9 that 'He ascended' must mean He had descended. If 'ascended' means Christ being taken up to heaven, then His descent must refer to His incarnation, that He emptied Himself, *taking the form of a servant, being born in the likeness of men* (Phil 2:7) and suffered extreme humiliation in the stead of His people. Where is Christ now? He is in where *far above all the heavens* (v10). It is not literally a place beyond the world but an authority higher than all this universe has known. In terms of His body and human presence, Christ is far from us, and yet the beautiful picture is that He is near (imminent) simultaneously because now *he might fill all things* by the power of His Spirit! In fact the reach of His presence now is far more than when He walked on earth. He said to His disciples that *it is to your advantage that I go away, for if I do not go away, the Helper will not come to you. But if I go, I will send him to you* (John 16:7).

7. **What were the gifts given to the early church (4:11)?** Each believer is unique with his gifts and church life is therefore diversity-in-unity. Individuals' gifts are embodied in the offices they take. Here Paul's focus is on 'word gifts', which are the foundation of building up a church. Ministries involve teaching and preaching the Word of God were *apostles, prophets, evangelists, pastors and teachers*. Briefly, *apostles* refer to the Twelve plus Paul, who were called by Christ as the sent ones on a mission. Their word was Christ's Word to people. They were authenticated 'by signs and wonders and miracles' (2 Cor. 12:12). Their ministry was broader and did not confine to one area. When the New Testament was completed and the foundation of the Church was laid, the office of apostle ceased. When they died out, they were not replaced. *Prophets* appeared to work exclusively within the local congregation. They always spoke of God but their message was judged by the apostles. A possibility could be that their message was more personal and practical while the apostolic teaching was more doctrinal and general. Similarly, the office of prophet is not needed today either because we have the Scriptures. We may think of *evangelists* as deputies to apostles and prophets, like Philip (Acts 21:8) and Timothy (2 Tim. 4:5). These men however were not evangelists in the sense we use the term today – with special 'evangelistic' gifts.

Pastors and teachers are ongoing ministries in any true church today. Here the two nouns are linked together by a single definite article (*the* pastors and teachers), leading to the view that it may mean pastor-teacher. Pastors surely must teach although teachers are not necessarily pastors. The word translated as *pastor* usually means *shepherd*. To qualify as a pastor, one must have a shepherd's heart to care and protect those entrusted to him. The office of pastor-teacher extends to that of the elders. They are the overseers of the entire church; they are to care and feed the church, as well as to protect the church with spiritual guidance. After the apostolic era came to a close, the office of pastor-teacher emerged as the highest level of local church leadership.

Church growth by God's plan (4:12-16)

8. **What is the single purpose of all these gifts and ministries (4:12)?** Word gifts are not for self-promotion but to build up the fellowship. They serve the single purpose of *equip[ping] the saints for the work of ministry, for building up the body of Christ*. The word *equip* was a medical term used in restoring broken limbs. It carries a meaning of restoring to its original condition or being made complete. Our true completeness and perfection depends on our being united in the one body of Christ. A church where saints gather is likened to a hospital for the sick people with sinful and broken lives. It is critical to note the centrality of the varied word ministries in this process of 'healing the sick' and 'building up the weak'. God's Word is the assigned means to restore lives to spiritual health and build up their spiritual strength and stamina for future service at church. God's way is through His Word being expounded faithfully and applied by the power of the Spirit in prayer so that it heals, cleanses and transforms our broken lives from sin to obedience. *Sanctify them in truth; your word is truth* (John 17:17). This sanctifying work of God's Word is intensive treatment, penetrating our minds, hearts and conscience to bring about universal obedience in all of

life. A church that neglects its word ministries is dire; it will not see spiritual health and consequently saints are not *equipped for the work of ministry*. 'The great need of the church has always been spiritual maturity rather than organizational restructuring... The first concern of the leadership of the church should be for the filled seats, not the empty ones.'[34] J C Ryle is right in that the Bible literacy of the laity is a measure of the spiritual health of a church.

9. **What is the fruit of ministry in a church (4:13-14)?** The vision is for the church as a whole through the working in the individuals. That isolated pockets of progress exist among members is not sufficient if the church as a whole lacks behind. The goal for the church has to be achieved *together until we all attain to* the following states:

- *The unity of the faith* – as in 4:5, *the faith* here refers not to our personal faith but to the body of doctrine revealed in the New Testament. Belief in *the faith* is not head knowledge only. Rather, it works through our whole body, recalibrating our minds, thinking, wills and desires to the mind and will of Christ (cf. 1 Cor. 2:16). <u>Members of the church will be more in tune with one another when each one of them tunes more and more to Christ. This is God's way to build up the horizontal unity in a church.</u> Tozer puts it beautifully:

    > Has it ever occurred to you that one hundred pianos all tuned to the same fork are automatically tuned to each other? They are of one accord by being tuned, not to each other, but to another standard to which each one must individually bow. So one hundred worshippers together, each one looking away to Christ, are in heart nearer to each other than they could possibly be were they to become

---

[34] MacArthur, John, ibid., p.154.

Session 7: Ephesians 4:1-16

'unity' conscious and turn their eyes away from God to strive for closer fellowship.

It denotes 'that closest union to which we still aspire, and which we shall never reach, until this garment of the flesh, which is always accompanied by some remains of ignorance and weakness, shall have been laid aside' (Calvin).

- The unity *of the knowledge of the Son of God* – as discussed above, *the faith* refers to the body of doctrine revealed in the New Testament, which in sum, is the truth about our Lord Jesus Christ. We have no other access to knowing Christ than the revelation given to us in Scripture of who He is, what His will is and what He has done. Without such knowledge, the danger is that we each follow a Christ forged in our own imagination. This is idolatry and not the Christian *faith*. Even though we call 'our idols' the same name, it does not unite! <u>Therefore, it is clear that an increase in and deepened *knowledge of the Son of God* builds up unity of the church.</u> Paul's point is that faithful word ministries of various kinds are foundational for church unity.

- Spiritual maturity (*to mature manhood, to the measure of the stature of the fullness of Christ*) – infants live on a milk diet. *But solid food is for the mature, for those who have their powers of discernment trained by constant practice to distinguish good from evil* (Heb. 5:14). The spiritual mature should be skilled in the word of righteousness and ought to be teachers (see Heb. 5:12&13). *Mature manhood* means having the fullness of Christ dwell in us, which is not separated from knowing well and being skilled in God's Word and letting it dwell richly in us through constant meditation and practice. Apart from Christ we are incomplete.

- Spiritual discernment and stability – the latest trends always have a pull on us, as if we were afraid of missing out on something big. We hate being seen as falling behind of our time or being old-fashioned. C. S. Lewis terms this as 'chronological snobbery'. Church is no difference, and easily falls into this trap, desiring to look 'relevant' to people outside in the way that people define it. It ends up being *tossed to and fro by the waves and carried about by every wind of doctrine, by human cunning, by craftiness in deceitful schemes* (v14). It is practically hard to be immune from the world and the values it promotes. After all, we want to be loving and welcoming. In an attempt to make the message 'appealing', the church may be listening to the people instead. Paul's warning to Timothy is timeless: *For the time is coming when people will not endure sound teaching, but having itching ears they will accumulate for themselves teachers to suit their own passions, and will turn away from listening to the truth and wander off into the myths* (2 Tim 4:3-4). Insidiously the philosophy of the world worms into the church, which begins to speak its language. An open Bible but with misinterpretation ends up cultivating a deceived mind. Maturity gives us spiritual discernment to see through *human cunning* and *craftiness in deceitful schemes* (v14), having the power to detect anything false and the foresight to see its danger if it is allowed to take root. Being heavy-weighted in *the stature of the fullness of Christ* (v13), we may be steady and stable, *no longer be children, tossed to and fro by the waves* (v14) that will undermine our unity.

10. What is God's way to church growth as opposed to human way (4:15-16)?

- *Speaking the truth in love* (v15) – (lit. 'truthing in love'). 'Truthing' may involve more than speaking. A church should be a fellowship of integrity with the truth as its base, exercised in the context of love. It rules out pretence and hypocrisy from the fellowship. It is not about any truth but the truth of Christ. Immediately we see the prerequisite would be for each of us to be thoroughly equipped in sound doctrine and in spiritual maturity – all the attributes that have gone before in verses 12-14. *Speaking the truth in love* is a difficult art to master especially when it is for reproof and correction from God's Word. Not only do we find ourselves ill-equipped with God's word to do it, against a culture of individualism and love taken to mean only affirmation, people often only hear criticism and rejection, not the truth, in reproof and correction. In the final analysis, the basis that enables us to *speak the truth in love* to each other is *the unity of the faith* (v12).

- God's way to church growth is <u>organic</u>. Growth will happen by itself when the right conditions are present. What are the right conditions? Paul uses the imagery of a body. The key is that all the body parts are individually connected to the head, knowing its mind and will: *we are to grow up in every way into him who is the head, into Christ* (v16). The body parts are pictured to be *joined and held together by every joint with which it is equipped* (v16), i.e. they are in close connection whereby spiritual supply, resources and gifts are passed from one member to another. When each of the members of the body functions properly with its assigned gifts to the church, healthy growth will take care of itself *in love*.

- Therefore, church growth is not a result of human schemes or clever methods to attract people to come in, with emphasis on the quantity at the neglect of the quality of members already in the pews. God's formula is this: 'every individual believer is to stay close to Jesus Christ, faithfully using his spiritual gift in close contact with every believer he touches, and that through such commitment and ministry the Lord's power will flow for the building up of the Body in love.'[35] There cannot be an active, united congregation, in biblical terms, if there is not love between its members.

Applications

'Attempting to build the church by human means only competes with the work of Christ.'[36] 'Why do we seek other models? Is it because we are so malnourished that we lack the appetite and the stamina [for an intense diet of the ministry of the Word]?'[37]

11. What has been 'the model' of <u>church fellowship</u> you have been taught? How does it match up with the biblical vision you have learnt from today's passage? Has the focus been in the right place?

---

[35] MacArthur, John, ibid., p.161.
[36] MacArthur, John, ibid., p.152.
[37] Ferguson, Sinclair (2005), ibid., p.111.

Session 7: Ephesians 4:1-16

12. What has been 'the model' of <u>church growth</u> you have been taught? How does it match up with God's way to church growth? Has the focus been in the right place?

13. Revisit the self-reflective questions at the beginning. In what ways would you approach church life differently following the study? Are you *worthy of the calling*?

14. How do you *speak the truth in love* at your church?

8. Radically New [4:17-24]

As discussed in the previous session, the second half of the letter to the Ephesians can be summed up by one exhortation which is given in 4:1: *to walk in a manner worthy of the calling to which you have been called*. But before Paul details what this *new* walk in our personal life looks like, he teaches us what this correction is for in 4:1-16. Surprisingly the aim is not for our personal enrichment or gain, to become nobler, lovelier and happier persons but for a higher purpose of maintaining the unity (4:3) in this new humanity which is *of the Spirit in the bond of peace* (4:3). This purpose was once hidden away as *the mystery of Christ* (3:4). This unity is how *through the church the manifold wisdom of God might now be made known ...* (3:10). That is to say, the gospel is broader than individuals being saved from God's wrath and the torment of sins; the ultimate goal of the gospel is a new united humanity created in Christ (2:15), which is made up of the redeemed individuals, to the glory of His name. This is why Paul starts the second half by instructing that believers must come together in this new community, an alien concept to both Jews and Gentiles. He therefore first dissects for our understanding its unique creation,

Session 8: Ephesians 4:17-24

its unique character of unity, its unique diversity of graces, its unique structure of life and its unique way of growth.

Following the comprehensive vision of the church, Paul zooms in on how every believer should live as its member with a series of imperatives. However, being Christians is not about what we do but who we are; our changed behaviour reflects the underlying changed nature. The drastic difference in comparison with what we used to be shows that this newness in believers is not something additional to our former nature but radical, i.e. a new nature of the core.

Self-reflective questions

What is God's most noticeable work in your character to date? How has the Spirit performed this work and what difference has it made in your life?

Alternatively, you may be brought up in a Christian home and grow up knowing the Lord from your youth. Are you troubled by not seeing a transformation in your life that you even doubt your faith? How do you know Christ lives in you?

Whom we are no longer (4:17-19)

1. **If we are to live out the divine purpose of the church, what must the members not do and how does Paul stress its importance (4:17)? Why does Paul turn back for a third time on how believers used to live?** We <u>must</u> *no longer walk as the Gentiles do*. Behind this, he puts his full weight of authority as an apostle of Christ. *Now this I say and testify in the Lord*. He speaks as the representative of Christ, so his words constitute the solemn and binding testimony of an apostle with his full authority. Having dissected how the church is held together (4:1-16), Paul next stresses that the walk of its individual members is the way how God is to manifest His grand vision.

   The emphasis is proportionate to how easy it is for us to fall back on our old way which is familiar to us and in turn tempting when we are off guard. <u>Keeping the Christian walk requires constant effort and attention</u>. Whenever we slack off on effort, our former way of life is our fallback position. That is why the Bible warns us against slothfulness. In this sense, a believer's new way of life is <u>about Christian discipline and habits</u>. It is particularly important to remind the Ephesians that they *must no longer walk as the Gentiles do*, because their old way of vice and corruption were everywhere around them and condoning immorality.[38]

2. **Who are the 'Gentiles' in 4:17? Compared with its usage in 2:11, what is the difference?** In 2:11, the Ephesians are identified as Gentiles while in 4:17, they are identified as distinctive from the Gentiles. Therefore, 'Gentiles' in these two verses cannot mean the same thing. In 2:11, *Gentiles*

---

[38] 'The fifth-century B. C. Greek philosopher Heraclitus, himself a pagan, referred to Ephesus as "the darkness of vileness. The morals were lower than animals and the inhabitants of Ephesus were fit only to be drowned." There is no reason to believe that the situation had changed much by Paul's day. If anything, it may have been worse' (MacArthur, John, ibid., p. 166).

Session 8: Ephesians 4:17-24

refers racially and ethnically to all non-Jews and in turn religiously to all pagans before Christ. As such, the Ephesians were part of them, and Paul refers them as *you Gentiles* in 2:11. But as the dividing wall between Jews and Gentiles has been abolished by Christ, *the Gentiles* in 4:17 refer to those who do not know God, here representing all ungodly, unregenerate and pagan persons. As the Ephesians are believers and have now been admitted into God's family, they are distinctive from *the Gentiles* in the second sense. While the pronoun for the Ephesians is *you* in the letter, 'the Gentiles' are now referred to as *they* in verses 17-19; the Ephesians must differ from unbelievers still trapped in their sinful condition – *in the futility of their minds*.

3. **What is the state of 'the Gentiles' (4:18)? What is its fruit (4:19)?** The logic of verse 19 works like this: *their hardness of heart* gives rise to their wilful *ignorance* which cuts them off from the life of God; being *alienated from the life of God* leads them to be *darkened in their understanding*. Paul gives a lengthier version of this teaching in Romans 1:18-32. The Bible teaches that with respect to the kingdom of God, and all that relates to the spiritual life, the light of human reason differs little from darkness. This initial blindness is the punishment of original sin. But it is *their hardness of heart* that condemns them. Their effort to solve the big questions of existence is doomed to be *futile*. Given that the knowledge of God is the true life of the soul, ignorance is the death of it.

The deadly fruit that is borne is their *callousness* (v19) – it means unfeeling, insensibility to pain or danger, no shame for their depravity, no fear of God or His wrath and no dread of the divine judgement. They have no awareness of their peril, and literally they would walk over the cliff in their laughter! When men persist in following their own way, their choice will eventually be confirmed by the God of heaven; because they would not believe, they could not believe. *Let the evildoers still do evil, and the filthy still be filthy* (Rev. 22:11a). Thus in their manner of walk, we observe there is a letting go without any regulation or restraints in the pleasures of sin; they *have given themselves up to sensuality, greedy to practise every kind of impurity* (v19). Such life is destined for eternal disappointment. As the standards of morality slip in our day, immorality becomes a shameless and callous way of life, not only made acceptable but even respectable and virtuous! There is no qualm in making money (being *greedy*) by promoting 'impurity'.

We are radically new (4:20-24)

4. **What have brought on the change in us; why are we different from *the Gentiles* now (4:21)?** We *have heard about him and were taught in him, as the truth is in Jesus*. Note the past tense (we <u>have heard</u> and we <u>were taught</u>) which points to a one-time past act. Paul tells us that *So faith comes from hearing, and hearing through the word of Christ* (Rom. 10:17). This *truth* that is *in Jesus* is not knowledge waiting to be absorbed into our system of beliefs or as a competitive school of thoughts, but <u>one that speaks of reality we cannot deny</u>. It is as revolutionary and radical as the truth Truman learned in *The Truman Show* (1998) that his whole life had been a lie. That truth planted in him the courage to overcome his fear of the 'open sea', to go to the edge of his 'world', to open the exit door and leave the studio, where his make-believe world was situated. Likewise, the truth in Jesus is an uprooting, life-changing event.

5. **What is the way that we *learned Christ* (4:20, 22-24)?** The *Gentile* way of verses 17-19, i.e. our old way in our unbelieving days, is NOT the way we <u>learned</u> Christ – again note the past tense. We 'learn about' or 'learn from' a person,

Session 8: Ephesians 4:17-24

but how do we 'learn a person'? We learn about or learn from someone when we, say, read his biography. We pick and choose what is relevant for us to learn while we maintain our distance at all times. Learning Christ is completely different. As He steps into our shoes by His incarnation, taking on our likeness, we are required to step into His shoes, walk the path He walked, love the way He loves, go to our own Garden of Gethsemane and partake His suffering in order to know Him and the power of His resurrection. <u>To learn Christ is to know Him intimately in our union with Him – forgetting self and abiding in Him and He in us,</u> *as the truth is in Jesus* <u>(v21). It involves our whole life.</u> 'The mark of the Christian life is to think like Christ, act like Christ, love like Christ, and in every possible way be like Christ.'[39] Self is dead. *The old has passed away; behold the new has come* (2 Cor. 5:17).

6. **In this changeover from old to new, what must happen in the process (4:23)? What is the substance of this renewal?** How we live reflects our beliefs and thinking. We act differently when we think differently. The gospel impacts on our minds before our conduct. We must be *renewed in the spirit of our minds*, with us being passive in this action. This renewal entails an understanding of what happens to us when we become Christians and its implications for our life and eternal destiny. In a nutshell, we are to come to grip with the old humanity under Adam we once were and the new humanity created in Christ we are now.

7. **What is the difference between the *old* and the *new* (4:22, 24)?** The old self *is corrupt through deceitful desires* (v22) because it is under the headship of Adam. Following his act of disobedience in the Garden of Eden, the image of God that was originally in him was severely marred. We were born in

---

[39] MacArthur, John, ibid., p.174.

him and inherit his corrupt nature, which is lived out in our lifestyle and destiny. But thanks to Christ, the old self belongs to our former way of life! As we put our trust in Christ, the ties that bind us to Adam are broken and we are now adopted as sons into God's family (1:5). We now belong to the new humanity under the headship of Christ (1:10, 2:15). Instead of corruption, *the likeness of God* (v24) is restored in us by Christ. The essence of our new self is not corruption through deceitful desires but *true righteousness and holiness* (v24) after God's image.

Righteousness relates to our fellow men and reflects the second table of the Ten Commandments (Ex. 20:12-17). *Holiness* relates to God and reflects the first table of the law (Ex. 20:3-11). As Christ has shown in the Sermon of the Mount, the law is spiritual; it concerns not merely outward decency but also inner purity; it speaks to the soul no less than the body. <u>A believer now possesses a new self, a holy and righteous inner person pleasing in the sight of God. This is the believer's truest and freest self</u>. As the original blueprint for man's life, the Decalogue is never obsolete; it tells us God's will for men even though Christ's works have abolished the ceremonial law of Moses and torn down the dividing wall that separated Jews and Gentiles (2:14-16).

8. **How do you understand this *newness of life* in a believer?**
   - *Putting off* and *putting on* employs the metaphor of garments. However, what we are changing here is not our clothes but our nature. *Putting off our old self* and *putting on our new self* depicts genuine repentance, a new life that demands a turn away from our sinful life and a turn towards holiness in the regeneration of the Holy Spirit.
   - The old self does not refer to the earlier part of our life. It is not like closing an old chapter and starting a new one in the same storyline. Rather, our old self is on one trajectory

Session 8: Ephesians 4:17-24

whereas our new self on another leading us to a completely different destiny. The old self refers to the influences and powers of the world our earlier life is subject to (2:2). Our new self is subject to a new master – our Lord Jesus Christ. Our allegiance has changed; we have been plucked up from the kingdom of darkness and planted in the kingdom of light.

- The new self is not an augmentation but a replacement of the old self. It is <u>a new birth</u> into the new humanity united in Christ; we are a new creation, even *partakers of the divine nature* (2 Pet. 1:4). It means putting to death of our old self and Christ demands our complete, not partial, surrender. This newness is not superficial or partial but radical and comprehensive.

- It is not only that we are made new as individuals but a whole new order of reality has arrived. Christ has ushered in the kingdom of God; we live in the future hope as our present reality through faith. The implication of this newness is beyond our imagination as the gospel is a message of cosmic proportions and it takes a lifetime to work out into our thinking and living out what it means.

Applications

9. What are the clear marks of Christ that you see in your life?

10. Is your surrender to Christ partial? Which part of you or your life have you kept back from the reign of Christ? What is your experience of 'partaking the divine nature'?

9. Newness of life [4:25-32]

Christian walk is like gardening. It takes constant effort to keep a garden in shape. Neglect produces thorns and thistles because the ground is cursed by sin (Gen. 1:17-18); that is, thorns and thistles are what the ground naturally produces now if it is not being worked at. This is why we see Paul in 4:17 emphatically commands the Ephesians not to slip back to their former way of life. All that it takes for 'thorns and thistles' to reappear in their life is for them to be off guard and slack in their 'gardening' effort. The corollary of that they *must no longer walk as the Gentiles do* (4:17) is that they *must* keep up the constant effort in walking in *holiness and righteousness* after *the likeness of God* (4:24), with the ongoing process of our minds being constantly renewed (4:23) and us constantly filled with the Spirit (5:18).

Paul sees the danger of Christians letting busyness of life crowd out the constant effort we need to make to stay in connection with Christ. And when we struggle to live out what we know and are discouraged, our inclination is to focus on what to do rather than on Christ. For example, if we find ourselves lacking patience, we try to work out how *we* can be more patient. This is relying on our strength to meet the mark which will not do. Instead, the answer provided by Paul in this letter is to look to Christ as in Chapters 1-3. So, when we lack patience, we meditate on Christ's patience from what He has done for us and find delight in it. Then somehow (i.e. by the Spirit's work) His character will seep through into our bones and marrow, and we find ourselves imitating Him, sometimes even without us being conscious of it. This is the gospel power working in us.

The text of this session starts with *therefore*: the changes in our conduct flow out from our <u>new</u> nature to manifest its character of *true righteousness and holiness* (4:24). We no longer live under the domain of sin but in the freedom of Christ. Christian walk involves *putting off* our old self and *putting on* our new self (4:22-24). It is a pattern of <u>*displacement* and *replacement*</u> (or *mortification* and *vivification*) (see Session 4 Q10). Having explained it in general terms, Paul naturally falls on to the subject of specific examples to demonstrate how this pattern works in real life. It is not surprising that the imperatives contain both don'ts and dos at the same time. The list given here is not for unbelievers in the quest of self-improvement because they do not have the gospel power working in them and have to rely on the 'old' self (the nature of Adam's race) to make these changes which is impossible.

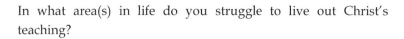

Self-reflective questions

In what area(s) in life do you struggle to live out Christ's teaching?

How have you been addressing the gap between your knowledge and your practice?

The manner of our walk (4:25-32)

Compare the old and new patterns of life in the following areas:

1. **4:25: Truth now replaces falsehood.**

    - **Who should speak the truth to whom?** Paul commands *each one of you*, that is, the believers, to *speak the truth with his neighbour*, whom Paul qualifies as *members of one another*. That is to say, Paul refers specifically to our conduct within the church here. It echoes 4:15 that we are 'truthing in love' to one another.

- **Why is it important to speak the truth to one another within Christ's body?** The truth is in Jesus (4:21). When we love Christ, we love the truth. Loving the truth and hating falsehood are the two sides of the same coin: *Therefore I consider all your precepts to be right; I hate every false way* (Ps. 119:128). If we embrace falsehood, Christ, being the truth, is forsaken and we go back to our former life. If we are indifferent to falsehood, we compromise the truth and not really love it. While truth has healing power, falsehood of any kind is like the invasion of viruses that causes malfunctioning in the body, damaging the health of the fellowship. The purpose of 'truthing' in love is for our spiritual growth into Christ who is our head (4:15). This is the way that the body of Christ grows organically, strengthened in unity, and builds itself up (4:16).

- **Application: why is it difficult to *speak the truth in love* (4:15)?** Truth without love can be harsh while love without truth is empty sentimentality. *A lying tongue hates its victims, and a flattering mouth works ruin* (Prov. 26:28). Against the beautiful lies, truth can be ugly to the hearer. There can be many reasons why truths can be offensive and in turn why we want to withhold the truth in fear of souring relationships with our brothers and sisters in church. It is especially so when in today's culture, we are expected to be 'nice', meaning not to confront or expose but to affirm. We do not listen well. These words are worth pondering: *Better is open rebuke than hidden love. Faithful are the wounds of a friend; profuse are the kisses of an enemy... Oil and perfume make the heart glad, and the sweetness of a friend comes from his earnest counsel* (Prov. 27: 5-6, 9). Trust is based on truth. It takes maturity to appreciate *earnest counsel* in fellowship as sweet and not sour. It also takes a lot of wisdom and spiritual acumen

Session 9: Ephesians 4:25-32

not only to know what to say but when and how to say it. *A word fitly spoken is like apples of gold in a setting of silver* (Prov. 25:11). *To make an apt answer is a joy to a man, and a word in season, how good it is* (Prov. 15:23)! Finally while everything we say should be unqualifiedly true, telling the truth does not mean that we tell everything we know with no regard for its impact. *Even a fool who keeps silent is considered wise; when he closes his lips, he is deemed intelligent* (Prov. 17:28). In some situations, silence, not honesty, may be love. Speaking the truth in love requires us to make all these judgement calls in our daily speech to one another.

2. **4:26-27: Righteous anger replaces sinful anger.**

   - **What would justify our anger?** Paul does not command, 'Do not be angry.' Rather, he says, *Be angry and do not sin.* If we genuinely love something, we cannot help but being angry at that which injures it. Jesus, for example, was angered when the Father's name was injured or others were mistreated. It is also right for us to abhor injustice, immorality and ungodliness of every sort, hating what God hates (e.g. Ps. 139:21-22).

   - **What does Paul caution us against in our anger?** Anger, even if it is just, easily gives *opportunity to the devil* to make us stumble in sin. Paul commands us to exercise restraints even with legitimate indignation.

   - **What is Paul's advice in dealing with our anger?** We should not let anger linger and let it master us: *do not let the sun go down on your anger.* The more time we let anger sit with us, the more bitterness and alienation is allowed to fester in our hearts. What started off as a concern for God's honour could become a personal crusade, losing sight of God. Paul is concerned that we should not allow the devil a foothold in our relationship with one another to stir up strife with rash words, ill feelings and self-justification. Furthermore, we should not be angry with our brothers and sisters in Christ but at their faults because in Christ they are already forgiven.

3. **4:28: Honest labour and generosity replace thieving.**

- **Do you steal?** We may not be criminals, but theft is more banal than we think. It is dishonesty, taking advantage of others or position for personal gain stealthily: for examples, pilfering office resources for personal use, padding expense claims, dodging customs, overstating hours worked, profiting from others' errors, delaying in paying your workers and so on. You get the idea.

- **What does Paul command a thief to do? What is the basis for this command (Gen. 2:15; 2 Thess. 3:10b)?** Paul commands a thief to stop stealing, *but rather let him labour, doing honest work with his own hands*. It is the creation mandate that man should work (Gen 2:15). Although work is toil and can be frustrating as a consequence of sin (Gen. 3:17-19), idleness does us much harm. We must be engaged in not just any work but *honest work*, i.e. God-honouring work. We should be responsible for our provision. Paul is direct when he commands elsewhere: *If anyone is not willing to work, let him not eat* (2 Thess. 3:10b). The goal in Paul's mind is not even so much as to provide for ourselves but *so that he may have something to share with anyone in need*. Generously we have received (from God in His abundant grace), generously we give. All that we have are gifts from God. In that sense, we are owners of nothing but stewards of everything. The question to ask as stewards is how God would want us to deploy His resources in our charge.

Session 9: Ephesians 4:25-32

- **Application: how would you discuss the rights and wrongs of the welfare state provisions?** It may be controversial to say this but living on welfare as a lifestyle choice rather than as a safety net for life mishaps of, for examples, ill-health or redundancy can be a kind of thieving – from taxpayers who toil in honest work to provide and from those who are in greater and genuine need. This is incompatible with a believer's new walk. Christian life is about giving and be generous to others as supported by honest labour of all who are able.

4. **4:29: Wholesome talk replaces corrupting talk.**

- **What are the principles of godly speech you can surmise from 4:29?**
    (a) Hold our tongue: *Let no corrupting talk come out of your mouth;*
    (b) What to say: *but only such as is good for building up*
    (c) How to say it: *as fits for the occasion;* and
    (d) Its effect: *that it may give grace to those who hear.*

- **Why must we hold our tongues and how easy is it to do so (Jas. 3:6-7)?** James leaves us with no illusions about the destructive power of our tongues. *And the tongue is a fire, a world of unrighteousness. The tongue is set among our members, staining the whole body, setting on fire the entire course of life, and set on fire by hell.* (Jas. 3:6). Words are powerful; they can build up or tear down, heal or harm; they can bring wisdom or folly (Prov. 18:21). James does not liken the tongue to a fire but that it *is* a fire. It starts small, spreads fast and soon goes out of control. It devours all things along its path, and its effects linger through *the entire course of life.* James' verdict is that *no human being can tame the tongue. It is a restless evil, full of* *deadly poison* (Jas. 3: 8). This is because *out of the abundance of the heart the mouth speaks* (Matt. 12:34) and our hearts are by nature sinful. To clean up our speech is to let our hearts be cleaned up by the Spirit through God's Word.

- **What does it take to fill our lips with wholesome talk?** Paul does not then recommend silence but to fill our lips with wholesome talk, which is a very demanding art to master on a closer look. It is not just about the content (*only such as is good for building up*) but also about the timing (*fits the occasion*). Filling up the content of wholesome talk will need knowledge (especially of the Bible as the foundation) which means a lifetime of study and learning. What should we meditate on? Paul has this advice: *Finally, brothers, whatever is true, whatever is honourable, whatever is just, whatever is pure, whatever is lovely, whatever is commendable, if there is any excellence, if there is anything worthy of praise, think about these things* (Phil. 4:8). To be able to say anything fitting for the occasion requires these words to be ready on our lips. That means *Incline you ear, and hear the words of the wise, and apply your heart to my knowledge, for it will be pleasant if you keep them within you, if all of them are ready on your lips* (Prov. 22:17-18). Further, saying the right things at the right time and in the right way, yielding the desirable impact of *giv[ing] grace to those who hear*, demands spiritual acumen which takes a compassionate heart and life experience to develop and mature over time. In comparison, holding the tongue may be easier than using it wisely for God's purposes! In sum, Proverbs describe wholesome in these words:

The wise of heart is called discerning,
And sweetness of speech increases persuasiveness.
….

Session 9: Ephesians 4:25-32

*The heart of the wise makes his speech judicious
and adds persuasiveness to his lips.
Gracious words are like honeycomb,
sweetness to the soul and health to the body.*
(Prov. 16:21, 23-24)

And we need to pray – for the effect of wholesome talk to take hold on the hearer.

5. **4:30-5:2: A pleasant and joyful dwelling for the Holy Spirit replaces one that grieves Him.**

   - **What is the relationship of the Holy Spirit with us (4:30)?** We have a close relationship with the Holy Spirit. He dwells in us. By Him, *you were sealed for the day of redemption* (v30). He is present as the sure evidence of our adoption. He also performs sanctification works in us. He is a person, someone who can be *grieved*.

   - **How do we *grieve* the Holy Spirit (4:30-31)?** Our corrupting talk grieves Him because it reflects the condition of our hearts. A Holy God does not like to live in our uncleanness. He is grieved also because we ignore His teaching and guidance, treating Him with contempt and making His works in us as if futile like ours. He loves us too and has our best interest at heart; it grieves Him when He sees us go astray to our own hurt in our foolishness and waste our potential to blossom in Christ.

   - **What does a pleasant and joyful abode for the Holy Spirit look like (4:31-32)? How is it possible to be found in us (5:1-2)?** Instead of what we should *do*, Paul closes this section by looking into what we should *be*, where kindness should replace animosity: *Let all bitterness and wrath and anger and clamour and slander be put away from you* *along with all malice. Be kind to one another, tender-hearted, forgiving one another, as God in Christ forgave you* (v31-32). In this inner being, the Holy Spirit will be at home because it is after the image of Christ. Christ has come and He is kind. His works have bridged the age-old divide and ended the deep-seated animosity. We have learnt so far in this letter that Christ has given birth to a new humanity characterised by unity rather than division, love rather than malice, peace rather than clamour, forgiveness rather than bitterness and wrath. <u>All that Paul asks of us is to look to Christ and be like Him</u>: *Therefore be imitators of God, as beloved children. And walk in love, as Christ loved us and give himself up for us, a fragrant offering and sacrifice to God* (5:1-2). More of that in the next section.

6. **How does our personal walk in this recommended way maintain the unity of the Spirit in the bond of peace (4:3)?** Chapter 4 opens with a vision for the church. Especially, the unity of the church is *of the Spirit in the bond of peace*. The Christian qualities that we see manifest in our calling and help maintain this unity spoken of are *humility and gentleness, with patience, bearing with one another in love* (4:2). Paul's imperatives for our personal walk in today's study are nothing but the outworking of these qualities needed for maintenance of this unity in the church.

Applications

7. What is your relationship with the Holy Spirit like? Do you have deep communion with Him?

Session 9: Ephesians 4:25-32

8. Which lesson(s) do you find most challenging in today's study and why?

9. Survey your relationships at home and at church. Has the study highlighted any specific problem areas for you to work on? If so, what are they and how may you work on them?

10. A New Gait: Love and Light [5:1-14]

How to *walk in a manner worthy of the calling to which [we] have been called* (4:1)? In the last session, Paul describes Christian living as *putting off our old self* and *putting on our new self* in practical terms, giving a list of dos and don'ts. It demonstrates that growing in grace involves the basic principle of *displacement* and *replacement* (or *mortification* and *vivification*) in our daily walk. When comes to the taming of our tongue (4:29), it becomes obvious that these standards are out of reach of the unregenerate. Jesus teaches that what comes out of our mouths reflects the condition of our hearts. Therefore, our corrupting talk will grieve the Holy Spirit of God who dwells in us. It leads Paul to tell us what should happen in our hearts, that kindness should replace animosity. All these imperatives converge to one focal point, that is, look to Christ, do as He has done and walk as He has walked – as the way *[we] learned Christ* (4:20). They are not moral codes snatched away from Christ for us to implement on our own effort. Chapter 5 opens aptly with the conclusion of the previous chapter: *Therefore, be imitators of God, as beloved children* (5:1). From that, Paul elaborates the guiding principles of

Session 10: Ephesians 5:1-14

Christian life: walk in love, walk in light, walk in wisdom and be filled with the Holy Spirit. At first glance, the specific imperatives may read as though they are repetitive but in terms of argument, Paul takes us to a higher level.

<u>Self-reflective questions</u>

Who do you take after, not in your outward appearance but in your manner of life? In what ways do you resemble this person? Why do you follow his or her example?

If you became a public figure and if journalists were going to dig into your past and present, what would they find that could give you bad press?

Walk in love (5:1-8)

1. **How do children learn to live (5:1 cf. 6:1-3)?** Children are mimics. It is only natural that they learn by imitating those closest to them, usually their parents. They learn by watching and sensing, as well as by hearing specific instructions and explanations. They are so observant that nothing escapes their watchful eyes. They are so absorbent that everything will be mopped up to form their intuitions. This is God's blueprint for human behaviour, as the Decalogue commands them to do so: Honour your father and mother (Ex. 20:12). This for very young children means obedience to their parents. Paul notes something special about this commandment: it is the first one with a promise *that you may go well and that you may live long in the land* (6:3). In fact, it is not the first but the only one with a promise. The promise is more profound than what meets the eyes. It means that obeying the parents is the training by God's design that will teach the children about all the other commandments, so the promise that they may go well. This is so because first their parents imitate their heavenly Father as His beloved children. We wonder what our new self is like. Look to God and we will know from His character who we are now as *partakers of the divine nature* (2 Pet. 1:4). Imitate Him and we know our walk, which ought to be different from that of the world and our past. This imperative is based on our Father-children relationship with God. The only way to know what God is like is to study His Word, which is His self-revelation. There is no other way.

2. **Who is the model of the pattern we are to imitate and what is this pattern (5:2)?** God reveals Himself fully in Christ, who is *the exact imprint of his nature* (Heb. 1:3). He is the God-Man, who makes the invisible God visible. He lived a life of perfect obedience to God the Father on earth. Christ Himself said,

Session 10: Ephesians 5:1-14

"Truly, truly, I say to you, the Son can do nothing of his own accord, but only what he sees the Father doing. For whatever the Father does, that the Son does likewise" (John 5:19). Christ did exactly what God has asked us to do here; He is the pattern for Christian living. Again, *[we] learned Christ* (4:20) through the pages of Scripture. There is no other way to know Him. However, if we attempt to live like Christ by our own effort, we will surely fail and be frustrated; rather, to live like Him is to allow the Spirit to pattern us after the Son.

This walk is characterised by love: *walk in love,* Paul exhorts, and this love is very specific in its quality after the example of Christ: *as Christ loved us and gave himself up for us, a fragrant offering and sacrifice to God* (v2). This is to distinguish it from the kind of love that the world promotes. Each age will have its nuances; for today, love is often equated with 'affirmation', even at the expense of truth, but as with all ages, it is always 'self-centred' and 'self-gratifying'. Given that Christ's love is of a different nature completely, it cannot even be directly compared with the love that the world offers. Christ loves us not because we are loveable but because He exercises His sovereign will to love us graciously. His love is characterised by faithfulness to His Word and mercy to the undeserving. <u>This highest love is self-forgetting, giving rather getting, *sacrificial* for the welfare of the object of love.</u> This love is *a fragrant offering to God* because it tirelessly works, sparing no expense, to bring the object of love ever closer to, rather than away from, God. This <u>godly</u> love is pleasing to God.

This character of Christ's love is not well understood in practice even within the church. One time a fellow member of the church said to me, 'My prayer has been that I could find some affection for you.' If we think carefully, this is the human way of love and its limitations. I acknowledged that this person did not like me very much and replied, 'Christ loves us not because we are loveable... If counting on myself, I would have little affection for anyone. Now I love first, so I have affection for people and not the other way round – this is how Christ's love has changed me.' It means whether I like the person is a non-factor. The body of Christ would be oiled up nicely if more understand how Christ's love works in practice and experience.

3. **What does Satan's counterfeit love look like (5:3-4)? What was the particular relevance to the Ephesians?** Love is an important makeup of our being. It has the power to shape and mould us. Love is a flow; outflow is sustained only by inflow. To love and to be loved are two sides of the same coin. For Christians, we love because God first loved us (1 John 4:19). In His perfect love, we are made whole and have no lack. His love for us becomes an inexhaustible fountain from which we are able to love others in a giving, selfless way following Christ's example. If people have to generate love from within themselves, love has to be <u>reciprocal</u> (giving in expectation of getting in return) and <u>conditional</u> (the object of love being loveable and attractive in some ways to arouse desire and affection). When love is reciprocal, it is not selfless; when love is conditional, it offers no sense of security. Without Christ's love, unbelievers attempting sacrificial love could lead to neglect of self. The psychological remedy is to put self first and learn to love self.

When we love the created more than the Creator, this love is *disorderly* or *unregulated* and in turn prone to excess. It is lustful, self-indulgent and self-gratifying. The quest for love becomes misguided and inevitably leads to *sexual immorality and all impurity* (v3), which are but forms of *greed* or *covetousness* (v3) driven by self-will, self-indulgence and self-gratification. Because of the strong sexual nature of human beings, sexual sins are powerful and can become perverted in unimaginable ways, masqueraded as something beautiful, desirable, good and rewarding. The force of these sins is so strong and attractive that people in pursuit of them are willing to sacrifice faithfulness to their promises and vows, happiness of their spouses and children, and the integrity of family and friendships. The havoc that disorderly love causes to individuals, families and society at large is incalculable. It is proper for saints to love purely as Christ, so these sinful acts *must not even be named among [them]* (v3), lest interest will be aroused in the sinful and saints be tempted. James has this insight that *if anyone does not stumble in what he says, he is a perfect man, able also to bridle his whole body* (Jas. 3:2). Given that our words are our thoughts and our thoughts are our words, the control over what we say and hear is more than an evidence of spiritual maturity; it is a means to it.

Sexual purity is a Christian discipline not only for the body but also for the mind. It is not sufficient that Christians should never engage in sexual sins; they should never entertain them in *filthiness, foolish talk,* or *crude joking,* which *are out of place* (v4), unfit for a holy fellowship that is filled with the *fragrant* aroma of sacrifice to God. This is a stark spiritual warning to the West, with its practice quickly spreading across the globe. The media daily bombard us with words and images of all things Paul lists to banish from saintly lives. Sexual sins are rampant as people, including Christians and churchgoers, are easily desensitized to the 'norm' of the society. Even if we do not engage in acts of sexual sins, what have we been allowing into our living rooms or on our phones as entertainment? Paul says these are out of place in a holy fellowship of God.

In Ephesus, sexual immorality and impurity spread not through media as in our day, but through their pagan worship. The height of pagan religious experience was communion with the gods through various forms of ecstasy. Heavy drinking (see v18) and sexual orgies were common practice to heighten sensation in the temple worship. Paul commanded his contemporary readers to walk away from this past life. This background is not dissimilar to our idolatrous lifestyle today.

4. **What is the remedy to unsanctified conversation and impure thoughts (5:4b)? What is the spiritual logic?** To combat these impure thoughts, Paul exhorts, *instead let there be thanksgiving* (v4). The spiritual logic is that when we see and appreciate everything in the light of Christ, love will be set in order, i.e. in the right relationships with Christ. <u>Orderly love will be in place of disorderly love and root out any undesirable wantonness</u>. And when we see and appreciate everything in the light of Christ, we see everything in its intended excellence and beauty, to which the only natural response is *thanksgiving* from deep down in our heart.

5. **Is Paul's pronouncement on the sinful harsh (5:5-6)? What could the deceiving *empty words* be in verse 6? What should genuine believers do (5:7)?** We are saved by grace alone (2:8) and all our sins are forgiven in Christ (1:7). On this offer, our sinful nature asks, *Are we to continue in sin that grace may be abound?* Paul rebukes this thinking categorically with *by no means* (Rom. 6:2)! Paul has been arguing in this letter that genuine faith is marked by <u>repentance</u>, the putting off the old self and the putting on the new self (4:22-24, see also S8Q8). A licentious lifestyle is evidence that the person under concern does not belong to the kingdom of God and in turn shares no inheritance with Christ: *For you may be sure of this, that everyone who is sexually immoral or impure, or who is covetous (that is, an idolater), has no inheritance in the kingdom of Christ and God* (v5). <u>Our depraved minds are skilled in self-</u>

Session 10: Ephesians 5:1-14

justification with warped reasoning in order that we are right in our own eyes. Paul implores us to watch out that we are not *deceived* by *empty words* (v6) that we would believe they are saved or God's grace is but a licence to sin – these are Satan's lies. Their lifestyle proves that they are *the sons of disobedience* storing up *the wrath of God* (v6).

Therefore, do not become partners with them (v7). To unbelievers, Paul warns them of God's wrath. To believers, however, Paul does not intend to alarm but rouse them to reflect, as in mirrors, the dreadful judgements of God that befall on *the sons of disobedience*. It would be unwise to fellowship with the ungodly whose ruin is sure. *Whoever walks with the wise becomes wise, but the companion of fools will suffer harm ... Leave the presence of a fool, for there you do not meet words of knowledge* (Prov. 13:20; 14:7). Paul reminds believers who they are now: *for at one time you were darkness, but now you are light in the Lord* (v8). Spiritually we now have nothing in common with the darkness of *the sons of disobedience*. We are no longer conquered by darkness; our task now is to invade darkness with light.

Walk in the light (5:8-14)

6. **What does it mean by *at one time, you were darkness* (5:8)?** This statement is staggering. We not only lived in darkness, but we were darkness. The darkness was not only outside but inside of us! We were not victims of darkness but its contributors, an element of darkness itself! When darkness is within us, we cannot tell darkness as darkness, but believe that it is light. How great is this darkness (Matt. 6:23) and what a tragedy! People generally process the world as evil outside them and in other people, so they can be disgusted by the state of affairs as if they were the innocent parties. Paul's blunt statement about us shatters that illusion. Darkness is

inside us and we are part of that darkness. But for believers, this was their past.

7. **Who are we now (5:8)? What is the fruit of our walk in light (5:9)? What is our guiding principle (5:10)?** In the Lord, we enter a new world and are under a new order of Christ. We <u>were</u> darkness but now we <u>are</u> light. The pattern of 'putting off' and 'putting on' appears here again. In verse 7, Paul calls us <u>not</u> to become partners with the son of disobedience, while in verse 8, he calls us to *walk as children of light*. A life in light should be widely different from a life in darkness.

There are two aspects to light: intellectual and moral. *For God, who said, "Let light shine out of darkness", has shone in our hearts to give the light of the knowledge of the glory of God in the face of Jesus Christ* (2 Cor. 4:6). The light of gospel shines on us and transforms our lives. <u>Light first works on our intellect to illumine our understanding and straighten our crooked thoughts.</u> In so doing, it drives out the darkness in our thinking, willing and feeling at the same time. Light turns around our moral conduct and produces the pleasing fruit *in all that is good and right and true* (v9).

The guiding principle is *to discern what is pleasing to the Lord* (v10). The word *discern* means 'the ability to evaluate.' 'Its background lies in the idea of examining and verifying something. It is used of examining metals in order to detect impurities and prove genuineness.'[40] How do we know what pleases God? God declares, *"This is my beloved son, with whom I am well pleased"* (Matt. 3:17). The life and ministry and obedience of Christ show us what pleases God. He came to fulfil the law rather than abolishing it. The moral law instead of condemning us now teaches us the character of God and

---

[40] Ferguson, Sinclair, ibid.., p. 133.

Session 10: Ephesians 5:1-14

His intended blueprint of mankind. <u>All that we need to know about how to please God is given in Scripture.</u> Therefore, to gain spiritual discernment, one must be well versed in Scripture. There is simply no shortcut or any labour-saving way. *'This life of discernment is, therefore, a Word-focused and Word-directed life, which develops a Word-saturated mind.'*[41] How can we be obedient when we do not know what the instructions are? Wilful ignorance is a sin.

8. **What is a key characteristic of *the unfruitful works of darkness* and what is the key property of light (5:11-14)?** *The unfruitful works of darkness* characteristically avoid light and are done *in secret* because they are *shameful*. <u>Darkness has no shame because they don't know what shame is and they think they could commit those works with impunity</u>. Proverbs shares this wisdom: *Whoever isolates himself seeks his own desire; he breaks out against all sound judgement; Stolen water is sweet, and bread eaten in secret is pleasant* (Prov. 18:1; 9:17). Jesus observes that *people loved the darkness rather than the light because their works were evil. For everyone who does wicked things hates the light and does not come to the light, lest his works should be exposed* (John 3:19-20).

Children of light should *take no part in the unfruitful works of darkness, but instead expose them* (v11). As light dispels darkness, they have nothing in common. Not only does light expose what is invisible, light is also what has been exposed and become visible. God's Word is light. Not only is God's self-revelation, it also searches and examines our heart, including all the secrets lurking deep within, things we did not know or did not want people to know. The Holy Spirit through God's Word exposes our sins and convicts us of them. But the goal is not in shaming but in bringing them into

---

[41] Ferguson, Sinclair, ibid., p. 134.

light also. Making sins *visible* (v13) to our consciousness makes us feel the weight of guilt and is a step towards our repentance. The deeds of the sons of disobedience are waiting to be exposed by the light. *For it is shameful even to speak of the things that they do in secret* (v12). Then they will hear the call of the Shepherd to *Awake, O sleeper, and arise from the dead, and Christ will shine on you* (added emphasis). They too come into the light of Christ and bid farewell to a lifestyle in darkness.

Application: how well are you shining as *light* in both words and deeds? (1) How effective is your Christian witness to others? Do you bring God's Word to people in their situations and does your lifestyle bear the light of the gospel that people may see? Do people know you are a Christian? (2) We may be better in not participating in the unfruitful works of darkness. But how well are we in exposing evil to light? I believe sin of connivance is a common sin of Christians. We cowardly watch people commit wickedness as bystanders and do nothing for fear of the repercussions on ourselves. A spiritual war is raging as Paul will discuss in Chapter 6. Augustine dissects our cowardice with these words:

> We tend culpably to evade our responsibility when we ought to instruct and admonish them, sometimes even with sharp reproof and censure, either because the task is irksome, or because we are afraid of giving offence; or it may be that we shrink from incurring their enmity, for fear that they may hinder and harm us in worldly matters, in respect either of what we eagerly seek to attain, or of what we weakly dread to lose.[42]

Exposing evil invites hostility from the wicked, which may cost us dearly, hence the hesitation. Although we are not

---

[42] St. Augustine (1467), *City of God*, translated by Henry Bettenson, Penguin Classics (2003), p15.

Session 10: Ephesians 5:1-14

facing atrocities as committed by the Nazis in the Second World War, how many social controversies of today are we engaged in by telling the truth to expose their follies? Paul is saying that knowing the truth ourselves is not enough but that we must use the light to expose *the unfruitful works of darkness*. This I believe is a challenge to many of us to do and to do it wisely (see next session).

Applications

9. A godly relationship is one that brings both parties closer to God. We do not naturally love like Christ. What has God done to set your love in order and what more do you think He may do?

10. What do you read; what do you watch? Do you enjoy sins of *the sons of disobedience* vicariously? What would be a godly principle in recounting sins (5:3)? What has God convicted you to do by this study?

11. Are you challenged by the property of light to expose *the unfruitful works in darkness*? What are the difficulties for you in doing so?

11. A New Gait: Wisdom [5:15-21]

Paul sees clearly the issues we face when we try to apply the property of being light to expose deeds done in secret (5:11-12). That *the days are evil* (v16) sums it up. Even quiet and consistent godliness can provoke deep anger and hostility in this evil world. It echoes Jesus' instruction to His disciples, *Behold, I am sending you out as sheep in the midst of wolves* (an image of the world as evil and dangerous for the *'sheep'*), *so be wise as serpents and innocent as doves* (Matt. 10:16). We need wisdom to navigate through the evil world without compromising our calling on the one hand and being devoured on the other. This is what Paul turns to address.

Self-reflective questions

In what area of your life do you find yourself wishing for wisdom? What are the difficulties?

Where do you look for wisdom?

Walk in wisdom (5:15-21)

1. **Why does Paul call us to *look carefully* (5:15-17)?** *Look carefully* (v15). We cannot expect to pass through the world absentmindedly without falling into harm's way because *the days are evil* (v16). Christian walk is full of intent, God's intent; it requires us to think carefully what we are doing and look that we walk on the right path. We also need to keep watching in case we wander off the path. We walk *not as unwise but as wise* (v15). The Hebrews understood wisdom to be skill in living righteously, 'the art of steering' through life. It involves knowing how to achieve the best ends in the best way. Therefore, while wisdom is not mere knowledge, there can be no wisdom without knowledge. What is 'right' or 'best' involves judgement or discernment (v10, see S10Q7) and a target to strive for. To settle these questions requires knowledge. For the wise, the 'right' target in life is to accomplish God's will; anything else is foolishness. *Therefore, to be wise is not [to] be foolish, but understand what the will of the Lord is* (v17). Paul wants believers *to be wise as to what is good and innocent as to what is evil* (Rom. 16:19).

2. **What does Paul mean by making *the best use of the time* (5:16)? How do we do that?** The Greek verb used here for *making the best use of* (ESV) or *making the most of* (NIV) is the same verb used by Paul in Galatians 3:13 where it is

translated as *redeemed*, in that Christ *redeemed* us from the curse of the law. Calvin therefore happily translates the verse as *redeeming the time*.[43] This presents a completely new dimension of understanding the verse. The idea is that we have to buy back the time if we are to use it wisely, but redeem from what and for what end? Paul tells us that we need to redeem the time *because the days are evil* (v16). We were born in the fallen world and in our fallen nature, which has the first claim to all of our time. Due to this corruption, our default time use is to 'chase after wind' (Ecc. 1:14) for the cares and pleasures of this world, for our vainglory and for self-indulgence. Even when we have become Christians, we are still locked in this mindset, being very protective of 'our' time and struggle to dedicate it to God. In this sense, time for the glory of God has to be bought back from the tyrannical hold of this 'present evil age' (Gal. 1:4).

The Greek word for *time* is not clock-time (the continuous time measured in hours, minutes and seconds). Rather, Paul uses a word that refers to an allocated fixed season or epoch.[44] Therefore, *the time* with the definitive article refers to God's set time for our lives and in turn our opportunity for service to Him. This is why NIV translates verse 16 as *making the most of every opportunity*. This principle has of course been demonstrated perfectly by our Lord Jesus Christ, who had no time to lose to do God's works while He walked on earth! In John 8:59, Jesus was on the run from the Jews who tried to stone Him and in the next verse (9:1), He stopped to heal the man born blind. He said: *We must work the works of him who send me while it is day; night is coming, when no one can work. As long as I am in the world, I am the light of the world* (John 9:4-5).

---

[43] See Calvin's commentary on Ephesians, available online.

[44] The Greek words are *chronos* and *kairos* respectively (see MacArthur, John, ibid., p.221).

This does not refer to the risen Lord but Christ as a man who was only on earth for *a day*, a very short period of time. His visit here below was the time for Him to work and He would not lose a second of it but grasp every opportunity to display the works of God (John 9:3). Likewise, we are here on earth for a season only; how many are our days is in God's hand. But life will be short even at the very longest. It is probing to ask ourselves: do we *make the best use of our time* because the sun will soon set and there is no postscript to our life!

Application: how do you make more time for God? Most interpret this question as 'let's see how I may squeeze time for God in my hectic schedule'. They are not aware of the fact that this is a wrong question to ask. This mindset treats God as competing ends for our time use and this simply will not do; God will always be crowded out. Instead, to make time for God is to have this revolutionary thinking that God owns all the time we have. As such, we have to scrap our original timetable and start again with God having the claim of it. God is the one who is doing the allocation of our time, not us. Only then will we always find time for God. *Making the best use of the time* therefore means something specific, that is, <u>we redeem the time from the worldly claim on it and dedicate it to God</u>. 'But with what coin can time be purchased for the glory of the Lord? <u>The price is the self-discipline</u>, which arises from a desire to glorify God in all things'[45] (added emphasis). Therefore, Christian life is a disciplined life.

3. **How do we *understand what the will of the Lord is* (5:17)?** This is a million-dollar question, isn't it? Life is full of decisions, big or small. To discern God's will is to <u>read our life in Scripture</u>. This requires us to be well-versed in Scripture, which teaches us all that we need to know. To hear

---

[45] Ferguson, Sinclair, ibid., p. 139.

Session 11: Ephesians 5:15-21

God's voice is to open the Bible and read it with a submissive heart. James gives us these 'hearing aids': *quick to hear, slow to speak, slow to anger* (with God or at His counsel) (Jas. 1:19).[46] Then we apply His Word to our circumstances and discern His fingerprints, as He leads us in the paths of righteousness through His Word and providences. There is an ongoing live dialogue in prayer between His Word and our present life. Even so, we don't have perfect knowledge about our past or future. At any one time, we must recognise that God's plan for us may not have been fully unfolded to enable us to move forward in confidence. Still we must move forward in faith, trusting in the Lord and not ourselves. Waiting upon the Lord is part and parcel of *wisdom*.

4. **Why did the Ephesians get drunk (5:18)?** One easy way to live foolishly and waste our time is drunkenness. People may drink or not drink for many reasons, and drunkenness is also a painful social issue that wracks the life of many individuals and their families. It is obviously worth of our concern and reflection. The Ephesians were familiar with drunkenness that was closely associated with the rites and practices of pagan worship. In particular, heavy drinking, together with sexual orgies and other practices, was an integral part to heighten the sensual ecstasy in communion with the gods. It probably was prominent in their lifestyle and they faced no censure for it prior to their conversion. Even though believers have been delivered from the dominion of sin once-and-for-all, drunkenness may still linger in their lifestyle like some severe 'withdrawal symptoms'. Paul's counsel is not to give way! The religious reason to get drunk is now removed as they participate in pagan worship no more. Paul calls drinking to the point of being drunk *debauchery* (v18) which

---

[46] For a more detailed discussion, see Kwok, Eunice (2023) *Look in the Mirror: A Study on James: Leader's Notes*, KDP, p.18.

they ought not to do. This is an artificial way to a sensation of happiness which does not last. It gives them delusions of reality. It excites lust and lowers inhibitions. It clouds their judgement, inviting themselves to act foolishly and shamefully. Not only is it incompatible with the Christian walk we have been talking about, it is also not *the best use of the time* (v16) for sure. A drunkard cannot even walk straight, let alone walk in love, light and wisdom. *Wine is a mocker, strong drink a brawler, and whoever is led astray by it is not wise* (Prov. 20:1). *Do not look at wine when it is red, when it sparkles in the cup and goes down smoothly. In the end it bites like a serpent and stings like an adder* (Prov. 23:31-32).

5. **What is the godly replacement for *debauchery* (5:18)?** For the godly, past drunkenness should be replaced by *being filled with the Spirit* (literally, *keep on being filled with the Spirit*). It is an imperative in present tense but passive voice. That is, the filling of the Spirit is not something that we do but that we allow to be done in us. Now it should be clear that being filled is not the same as possessing. Every believer is indwelt by the Holy Spirit permanently at the moment of conversion. When we possess Him, we possess Him in full. Being filled therefore does not describe a process whereby we receive Him progressively by degrees or in doses. Rather, <u>it means our continuous submission to the truth of God's Word and its teaching under the Lordship of the Spirit. It produces a life of obedience to the will of God</u>. Being filled with the Spirit is not optional but a mandate for a believer because we can do nothing apart from God. It is like a glove which can do nothing unless it is filled by the hand. It is an ongoing, continuous submission to the Spirit's Lordship. Whenever we are not filled with the Spirit, we will fall back on living in our carnal nature, producing stunted growth, spiritual weakness, frustration and defeat.

Session 11: Ephesians 5:15-21

6. **What are the expressions of a Spirit-filled life (5:19-21)?** The Spirit puts a new song in our hearts, a song of faith and salvation that is given by God and not by the world. *Melody sung is directed to the Lord* (v19). However, we are also to *address one another in psalms and hymns and spiritual songs* (v19). Our singing in worship has both vertical and horizontal dimensions. Note that singing worship songs is not necessarily an act of worship. The key element is being Spirit-filled and sung *with your heart* and *to the Lord* (v19). If singing is from our lips and throat only, it will be an abomination to God. Singing alone at home is different from singing in a congregation at a worship service. When each of us, <u>filled with the Spirit,</u> sings praises to the Lord, we are elated and encouraged to hear the same devotion multiplied manifold in each other. That is when congregational singing <u>with one voice and one heart</u> *to the Lord* is glorious and can blast the roof off on its way to heaven!

Being Spirit-filled causes our hearts to be bursting with thanksgiving, *giving thanks always and for everything to God the Father in the name of the Lord Jesus Christ* (v20). When? *Always.* For what? *Everything.* Being thankful is an inexorable response to the abundant grace God has lavished on us (1:3-14). <u>Ingratitude is incompatible with Christian walk</u>. We are thankful for God's blessing (both temporal and spiritual), for our salvation and eternal hope, and for the purpose in our tough time of suffering and affliction. Truly we can be thankful in all circumstances and gratitude gives us joy in the heart. This peace of God surpasses all understanding (Phil. 4:7), making Christians distinctive.

A mark of being Spirit-filled is true humility, which is the first step to church unity and the root of every Christian virtue (see discussion in S7Q4). This is expressed in our *submitting to one another out of reverence for Christ* (v21), which is fundamental in maintaining the unity of our fellowship (see 4:3). To submit here is, literally, 'to line up under' – as in soldiers lining up under their general. This submission to one another within God's family is not one of power but love which is self-forgetting in the service of others. Such love is *out of the reverence for Christ* and after His example. As all godly persons are under the reign of Christ, no suppression or oppression underpins Christian submission to one another, and no one will take advantage of his position for personal gain. This principle is not only fundamental in our fellowship at church but also in all our earthly relationships as Paul expounds in the next section.

7. **Application: in light of Paul's teaching here, has your opinion been altered on what songs are appropriate for church worship? If so, how?** The subject of music at church has been a great controversy of our time. Books have been written on the debate, so it is impossible to give a comprehensive overview here. The purpose here is personal reflection. Today, churches may have the mindset of distinguishing worship service by their music, for example 'traditional' versus 'contemporary'. There are people who come to church for its music. It has increasingly become the focus of a worship service, which arguably is misplaced. Some churches seem to see music as the way to attract people to come in, as if they have lost their confidence in the gospel message itself. In some services, we see the extreme where music dominates to produce moods of worship, spirituality and transcendence without words, which again is off focus as to what worship to our God is about. Many think that music is down to personal taste which has no right or wrong. As long as the worshippers 'enjoy' the service, there is nothing to debate about. All along we miss the fundamental point that worship is to please God; it is for God to 'enjoy' rather than us. Therefore, it should be God's 'taste' that matters, not ours.

Session 11: Ephesians 5:15-21

To settle the question of what songs are appropriate for a worship service, we should not be debating on our personal taste but God's. It means we have to look for answer in God's Word, through which He reveals Himself to us. 'The Word of God is the test which discriminates between his true worship and that which is false and vitiated. His Word is employed as a bridle to keep us in unqualified obedience.'[47]

Here is Augustine's personal reflection on worship music on him, which I think provides some guiding principles for us too: 'there are particular modes in song and in the voice, corresponding to my various emotions and able to stimulate them because of some mysterious relationship between the two. But I ought not to allow my mind to be paralysed by the gratification of my sense, which often leads it astray.' He tells if he sins with music by this distinction: 'when I realise that nowadays it is not the singing that moves me but the meaning of the words when they are sung in a clear voice to the most appropriate tune, I again acknowledge the great value of this practice… Yet when I find the singing itself more moving than the truth which it conveys, I confess that this is a grievous sins, and at those times I would prefer not to hear the singer.'[48] Augustine's deliberation suggests that words are the element of worship while music is only an aid to worship. The words, which convey the gospel truth, set in the most appropriate tune should drive our emotions and not the music *per se*. Admittedly, this distinction is sometimes subtle, but for sure, we should question the role of pure music without words in a worship service. Secondly, lyrics are a crucial element of a song and they should be doctrinal and rich in biblical truths in order that we know without

---

[47] Calvin, *the Institutes of the Christian Religion*, translated by Henry Beveridge (2008) Hendrickson Publishers, 3:24:17.
[48] St. Augustine, *Confession*, translated by R. S. Pine-Coffin (1961), Penguin Classics, Book X Chapter 33.

ambiguity the God we are singing to. If this is not the case, the congregation can hardly sing with one voice and one heart and to the Lord (see Q6 above). Calvin adds: 'Songs composed merely to tickle and delight the ear are unbecoming the majesty of the church, and cannot but be most displeasing to God.'[49]

Applications

8. What have you been spending your time on? What or who has got claims on it? Can you improve on your time use according to 5:16 (see Q10)?

9. Do you drink? What are your principles on alcohol consumption (see Q12)?

---

[49] Calvin, *the Institutes of the Christian Religion*, translated by Henry Beveridge (2008) Hendrickson Publishers, 3:20:32.

12. Husbands and Wives [5:22-33]

Instead of getting a sensation of fake spirituality through drunkenness like the pagans do, Paul commands us to be filled with the Spirit constantly (5:18). This follows the same pattern of *putting off* and *putting on* in our Chrisitan walk. Among the expressions of being Spirit-filled is our mutual submission to one another (5:21), which is not one of power but true humility, characterised by love which is self-forgetting in the service of others after Christ's example (5:1-2). Such love is *out of reverence for Christ* (5:21). As all godly persons are under the reign of Christ, there ought not to be suppression or oppression in any relationships and in turn our submission should not be exploited. This principle is not only fundamental in our fellowship at church but also in all our earthly relationships as Paul expounds in this section.

Paul constantly exhorts us to forgo our former way and to walk in the new way of life. The newness in us is of a new order (the new humanity formed under the headship of Christ) and of another kingdom which is of heaven rather than of earth. Our transformation as believers is radical. As we have a new nature, the way we relate with others would change accordingly. Paul here describes the new vision for our earthly relationships associated with our new nature, which should be as revolutionary to the first-century Christians as to us today because the need to *put off* our old self and *put on* our new self is timeless. Paul's teaching is as controversial today as yesterday; contrary to our beliefs, we have not evolved into a better version of ourselves over time. Paul's first stop is the relationship between husband and wife.

Self-reflective questions

What model of marriage has yours been based on? Has it worked?

How have you worked to improve it?

Session 12: Ephesians 5:22-33

Wives submit (5:21-24)

1. **Why is this passage hard on the modern-day ears? Is God out of date? Is Paul chauvinistic?** In a society that hails gender equality (often taken to mean 'sameness') as an absolute and core virtue, many women, both in and out of the church, stumble over this passage that exerts gender difference. I have come across angry women using Paul's teaching on women to challenge the authority of the Scriptures or to justify their outright rejection of the Christian faith. To many women at church, this is still a thorny issue that we have been struggling with at both personal and corporate level as Christ's body. To keep peace, the subject is often avoided or left ambiguous to encompass a wide range of views. Since God is always right, the controversy and its heat simply show how far and successful Satan has been in defacing God's vision for family. Even believers are not exempt from being tainted by the worldly view. Talking about unity, it is worth noting that women's role at church is one issue that has enough weight to split a church. Since the issue at heart is women's submission to their own husbands at home (and male leadership at church), I wonder if our finding Paul's teaching difficult is precisely a symptom of our non-submission to God's authority. To listen well, we need true humility before God *to take captive of every thought to obey Christ* (2 Cor. 10: 5). As a woman at church, a wife and a mother at home myself, I have my own personal journey to tell as I learn obedience. I believe that the difficulty lies in the worldly value being deep-seated in our woman identity, which has effectively blinded us from seeing God's truth and hardened our hearts to accept it. It may take years for the Spirit to slowly chisel that blindness and hardness away before we may celebrate God's blessing in gender distinctions. One thing for sure is that Christianity does not put women down. Quite the

contrary, while Christ walked on earth, He treated women with attention and dignity that was counter-cultural in His day. And Christ is always our perfect example. What we are working against today is also the narrative that not only blurs but totally denies any gender distinctions, causing chaos in all our interpersonal relationships! May the Lord let Christ as light shine into darkness (5:13-14).

2. **How do we understand the battle of the sexes from Scripture (Gen. 3:16)?** The battle of sexes seems to have been a perennial fixture in human life! It shouldn't surprise us as it is a feature of our fallen world, the origin of which can be traced back to Genesis 3. In the Garden of Eden, Eve listened to the serpent and disobeyed God's command. In the process, she failed to consult Adam on the matter as she should. As a consequence of sin, God issued a list of curses. To Eve, He said: *Your desire shall be for your husband, and he shall rule over you* (Gen. 3:16). This *desire* is not sexual or emotional but one that compels women to take control in a marriage.[50] It means that since the Fall, woman's desire is to usurp the place of man's headship and man would resist that desire by ruling over her like a despot. It gives rise to the battle of the sexes we observe down the ages in its different forms. Throughout history and in some cultures of our day, the dominant distortion of relationships has been on man's side whereby women have been treated appallingly! Sin has brought an alien and divisive influence into relationships, most notably in marriage and family. Sadly, disharmony, brokenness and negligence rule in many

---

[50] The Hebrew word translated as *desire* in Genesis 3:16 appears in the next chapter verse 7: *If you do not do well, sin is crouching at the door. Its desire is for you, but you must rule over it.* God was telling Cain that sin wanted to master him, but he must master sin. The word translated as *desire* 'comes from an Arabic root that means to compel, impel, urge, or seek control over.' In this context, a woman's desire for her husband is not sexual or emotional but about power. (See MacArthur, John, ibid., p. 273.)

homes today. It takes the works of Christ that tore down the wall of division to restore the created order and harmony of proper submission and authority in a relationship that has been seriously defaced by sin. Paul's teaching here is a radical lesson for everyone in all ages.

3. **What were the norms of marital relationships in Paul's day?** In the New Testament times, the status of Jewish women was not much higher than servants. Many Jewish men prayed each morning: 'God, I thank you that I am not a Gentile, a slave or a woman.' God's law on divorce and remarriage had also been so twisted that a husband could divorce his wife at whims on the most trivial grounds. In contrast, divorce in Greek society was so rare that there was not even a legal procedure for it. This however was not a picture of 'true love' and 'happily ever after'. On the contrary, Greek men saw little reason to divorce their wives because concubines were common and marital infidelity was widely accepted on both sides. A wife's role was to bear legitimate children and keep house. Sexual promiscuity and perversion of various forms were therefore rampant in the society, inevitably leading to sexual abuse of children also. In Rome society, easy divorce which could be invoked as often as desired eroded marriage to be little more than legalised prostitution. Women did not want to have children and the desire to do everything men did grew into strong feminism.[51] All these issues that undermine marriage are eerily familiar to us today. We have not done any better than first-century people in protecting marriage. If anything, we have done the worst thing in redefining it! Against such backdrop, Paul's teaching concerning marriage is as revolutionary in his day as in ours!

---

[51] Based on MacArthur, John, ibid., p. 273.

The Making of Living Stones

4. **Some commentators suggest that verse 22 should be read in context of verse 21. How does verse 21 qualify the command to wives in verse 22?** In verse 21, mutual submission flows out from the *Spirit-filled* life of believers into all interpersonal relationships. It means that <u>all believers are spiritually equals in every sense</u>, and our submission to one another is *out of our reverence for Christ* (v21). It should be filled with love as Christ has loved us. It means that to live out Paul's command requires us <u>to be Spirit-filled</u> or it is hopeless. But as we often lapse in our willingness to be filled with the Spirit, we should not be surprised that our relationships ebb and flow accordingly. Even though relationships require constant hard work and at times frustrate us, their basis and vision are unchanged.

5. **How do we understand the submission of wives that Paul calls for (5:22-24 cf. 1 Cor. 11:3 and 5:32)?** In the original Greek, verse 22 has no verb; its verb is implied from verse 21. That is, the more literal translation would read: 'submitting to one another in reverence/fear of Christ ... the wives to their own husbands'.[52] This suggests that the verb 'to submit' is reflexive, and NIV makes this explicit: *Wives, submit <u>yourselves</u> to your own husbands as you do to the Lord.* It means that it is not the husbands' job to make wives submit to them; rather, the volition to do so comes from the wives themselves. Being equal before God does not mean that there is no hierarchy in relationships. As Paul explains, *the head of every man is Christ, the head of a wife is her husband, and the head of Christ is God* (1 Cor. 11:3). The Son is submissive to the Father in function while equal to the Father in nature and essence. Similarly, wives are to be submissive to their *own* husbands while completely equal to them in moral and spiritual nature. But this is not how we naturally see it. In

---

[52] Ferguson, Sinclair, ibid., p. 148.

Session 12: Ephesians 5:22-33

fact, the world's view is so ingrained in us that it is our default thinking without us noticing. We naturally think the one put over us is superior while the one to submit is inferior because we think wrongly that the one in charge has more freedom and can do whatever he wants and uses the position to exert superiority. This may be what it was like in a Christless relationship but is no longer in a Christ-centred one. Now in all relationships, we serve one common Master, who is Christ. As such the Bible hails a different definition of equality which does not mean 'sameness'. While men and women are equal, husbands and wives are called to different but complementary roles in the family structure.

Moreover, we have to understand the described relationship in the context of verse 32. Paul says the husband-and-wife relationship is a profound mystery and it *refers to Christ and the church* (v32), not only as groom and bride but also as head to its body (v23). First, as Christ is the head of the church, God has given husband authority over his wife as her head. Second, Christ is the saviour of His body for her best interest and security. As such, wives and husbands mirror different dimensions of the relationship between the Lord and His people. On the one hand, husbands' calling is to love their wives as Christ loves the church (see below). On the other hand, wives' calling is to illustrate how believers (His church) respond to Christ's love with deep and joyful submission (v24) as their saviour (v23): wives are to submit themselves to their own husbands *as to the Lord* (v22). Moreover, the scope of this union is total and complete, so *wives should submit in <u>everything</u> to their husbands* (v24).

Finally, this is <u>not</u> a general call that women submit to <u>all</u> men in the society. Paul is specific in that wives are to submit to their *own* husbands. It is a domestic, not a social, arrangement.

Husbands love (5:25-31)

6. **How are husbands to love their wives (5:25-27)? Who have the more demanding role in marriage, husbands or wives, and why?** Today's society often judges the demand Paul makes on wives to submit to their own husbands as unreasonable, if not downright offensive. On that basis, Paul's vision for marriage is easily rejected. In comparison, little spotlight is shone on Paul's demand on husbands! When we look closely at what Paul asks of husbands in marriage, it will quickly diffuse the concern that Paul has asked the impossible of wives.

Husbands are called to love their wives as Christ loves the church. This is a tall order! But as believers are partakers of the divine nature (see S8Q8), God would provide what is needed for husbands to love their wives with a measure of Christ's own kind of love. Christ displays the highest love for His bride (the church), which is self-forgetting, giving rather than getting, and sacrificial for the welfare of the bride. He loves His bride not because she is loveable but because He is faithful to His promise, making His love unbreakable. The basis of marriage is this covenantal love. By *[giving] himself up for her* (v25), Christ might separate her to be his own – that *he might sanctify her* (v26), i.e. to set apart. His mission is to beautify His bride and make her holy, splendid and spotless, i.e. loveable in His sight – *so that he might present the church to himself in splendour, without spot or wrinkle or any such thing, that she might be holy and without blemish* (v27); just imagine that presentation! For that, Christ did not just live but also suffer, humiliated, and die. She is cleansed *by the washing of water with the word* (v26). This does not refer to baptism by minister but the supernatural birth, our spiritual regeneration done by Christ Himself. Jesus told Nicodemus about this new birth that *unless one is born of*

Session 12: Ephesians 5:22-33

water and the Spirit, he cannot enter the kingdom of God (John 3:5). In same way, the commitment of a husband is to bless his wife through and through.

7. **How does Paul further argue that it would be unnatural for a husband not to love his wife (5:28-31)? How is this after Christ's example?** Marriage is a creation order, an institution set up by God. Eve was formed out of the substance of Adam and therefore of his bones and of his flesh (Gen. 2:23). Husband and wife are to become one flesh (v31). This union is unbeatable by any other earthly relationships in its intimacy; children are expected to cleave their parents in order to form this marital union (v31). Paul commands husband to love his wife as his own body (v28). Hating one's body is a psychotic behaviour. Similarly, it would be unnatural, even monstrous, if a husband hates his wife (v29). Put differently, Paul is teaching that no man can love himself without loving his wife! The marital union between husband and wife is the closest comparison we can get for the bond between Christ and His body (the church). Even so, the latter is closer still as the church is Christ incarnate! Christ abides in us as we abide in Him. Christ and His church are the Ultimate Couple, a marriage made in heaven, forged on earth but will last into eternity. *Because we are members of His body* (v30), Christ naturally *nourishes and cherishes it* (v29).

A profound mystery (5:31-32)

8. **What is a *profound mystery* in 5:32? How does Christ be in its midst to bless it (5:33)?** Record that a mystery in bible language refers to a secret that can be known only when God reveals it (see S2Q6). Paul quotes from Genesis about marriage in the previous verse, that *a man shall leave his father and mother and hold fast to his wife, and the two shall become one flesh* (v31). This union is a shadow of the relationship

between Christ and His church: *it refers to Christ and the church* (v32). As such, it remained a mystery until the reality of Christ and His church reveals it. Then we realise the *profound* meaning of marriage as it points to God's cosmic plan of 1:10 and 3:6!

As they mirror each other, marriage helps deepen our understanding of our relationship with Christ and vice versa. Marriage is hard; even two good people with the best intention in the world can and do fight! Many give up their marriages on the basis of irreconcilable differences or no-fault divorce. This is a far cry from Christ's covenantal love for His bride which is unbreakable: *For I am sure that neither death nor life, nor angels nor rulers, nor things present nor things to come, nor powers, nor height nor depth, nor anything else in all creation, will be able to separate us from the love of God in Christ Jesus our Lord* (Rom. 8: 38-39). For Christians, we find the secret of the life and quality of a marriage in our personal relationship with Christ. As we grow in Christ individually, we live it out in the marriage and make it stronger too. In marriage, no one should expect no change. We are His workmanship (2:10). As Christ continues to work in us, changes are what we expect and our marriage evolves with us. The conclusion is that *let each one of you love his wife as himself* (v33), i.e. look to Christ and imitate Him in your love for your wife (5:1). Then *let the wife see that she respects her husband* (v33). If your husband loves you as Christ does, why wouldn't you submit to him? One may submit but without respect. May husband be worthy of his wife's respect.

9. **Application: Is wives' act of submission dependent on husbands' love?** Given the opportunities that women have today, they are smart, strong, resilient and independent. To submit to their husbands is truly an act of volition and not of necessity as in the past. In contrast, it is well-known that it

Session 12: Ephesians 5:22-33

takes longer for a boy to grow into a man. The turning point for this transition often is responsibility. The day when a boy steps up to shoulder responsibility, his transformation into a man begins. In the past, it was usually the desire to get married that triggered the transition. Today, strong position of women retards their development. Together with the social narrative of toxic masculinity, the social trend is that men are at a loss in their gender role. We then end up in a catch-22 situation: wives do not want to submit because they don't trust their husbands as head of the family (yet), while husbands cannot or will not rise up to the role when they are not demanded to do so. Would wives step back in order to let their husbands take their God-assigned role in the family and in turn be shaped and developed by it? It benefits no one if husbands are left ineffective and do not fulfil their godly role. The discussion of the subject with younger women leads to the groan that it will be at their own hurt before husbands are ready. But on the principle of <u>mutual sanctification</u> in a marriage, they accept that the key to breaking the catch-22 situation probably lies with them.

Applications

10. If you are a woman, do you have or foresee to have trouble submitting to your husband? Why?

11. If you are a man, does the expectation to love your wife as Christ loves His church or as your own body make you nervous about marriage? If you are already married, what is your reflection on your role and what would you bring to prayer to the Lord?

12. What aspects of marriage still puzzle you? Where would you look for answers?

13. Children and Slaves [6:1-9]

Paul's message is that we have been made new in Christ and we have a new walk. From now on, Christ-centred relationships should replace the Christless ones before. The latter are bound by *disorderly love* in the sense that it serves to move and keep each other away from Christ. Paul instructs us to *take no part in the unfruitful works of darkness* (5:11). In our new manner of walk, this must not continue but be replaced by *orderly love* after the image of Christ (5:1-6). Love is directional and orderly love always directs to Christ for both the giver and receiver of that love. As light shines through darkness, it should transform all our earthly relationships into godly ones, yielding *the fruit of light [which] is found in all that is good and right and true* (5:9).

But what does a Christ-centred relationship look like? This is the focus of Paul in the second half of chapter 5. It is clear to Paul that interpersonal relationships start from home. Once we master those key and most trying ones, we will be able to master the lesser ones! A person's true spirituality is reflected not so much by how he presents himself in public but how he treats his family behind closed doors at home where his truest self and his true manner of walk is revealed. It is therefore not surprising that Paul lists the state of one's household as a key qualification of a church leader. *[An overseer] must manage his own household well, with all dignity keeping his children submissive, for if someone does not know how to manage his own household, how will he care for God's church* (1 Tim. 3:4-5)? And again: *Let deacons each be the husband of one wife, managing their children and their own households well* (1 Tim. 3:12). Anyone who has been a mother or a father would know children do not automatically fall in line! Rather, they reflect our very own rebellious spirit against God, which needs to be tamed, testing to its limit our knowledge, wisdom and commitment to God. In the last session, we studied Paul's instructions for husbands and wives. In this session, we continue our study on relationships for the rest of the household, namely, children and slaves. It takes two to tango, so it is Paul's pattern to address both sides of a relationship.

Self-reflective questions

What are your relationships with your children or your parents like?

How do you treat your hired hands?

Session 13: Ephesians 6:1-9

How do you treat your job?

Children obey (6:1-3)

1. **How does Paul justify that children should obey their parents (6:1-3)?** It is worth reminding ourselves that Paul is addressing believers in this letter, laying out God's blueprint for their family after their conversion, how they are not what they once were. His command for children is thus specified by *in the Lord* and in believers' households, God rules over all aspects of life! *Children, obey your parents in the Lord, for this is right* (v1). God is the one who defines what is right and what is wrong. It is right for children to obey their parents because God has ordained it to be so. The word translated as *obey* literally means 'to hear under'. Children therefore are expected to listen attentively and respond positively to what their parents say, i.e. they are put under the words and authority of their parents.[53]

God's approval of it can be found in the Ten Commandments, all of which are stated in negatives except two. The exceptions are the fourth commandment to keep the Sabbath and the fifth one to *honour your father and mother* (v2). The latter is the first one of the Second Table of the Law which governs our relationship with others, as opposed to the First Table, which governs our relationship with God. Paul further points out that *this is the first commandment with a*

---

[53] MacArthur, John, ibid., p.311.

promise (v2). In fact, it is not the *first* one but the *only* one with a promise. The promise is *that it may go well with you and that you may live long in the land* (v3). What is the spirit of this law to children then?

The Ten Commandments are written to ward us off our sinful tendencies and point us back to God's image in which we were created. It means that disobedience to parents is in children's sinful tendency. The natural order is such that children belong to their biological parents; that is, children's first ever relationship is with their parents. In God's design, parents are the conduit of His blessings to the children, both temporal and spiritual. As such, obedience to their earthly parents would teach children obedience to God, their heavenly Father, that is everything to render the promises of the Lord's blessing true in their life. That is to say, in obeying this command, a child soon learns what all the other commandments mean, and blessing will come through in the form of life and wisdom. *Hear, my son, your father's instruction, and forsake not your mother's teaching, for they are a graceful garland for your head and pendants for your neck* (Prov. 1:8-9). *Keep hold of instruction; do not let go; guard her, for she is your life* (Prov. 4:13). *Whoever ignores instruction despises himself, but he who listens to reproof gains intelligence* (Prov. 15:32).

It should be noted that the fifth commandment is to *honour* our parents, which is a broader idea than to *obey* our parents. *Obey* is to do with action while *honour* is to do with attitude. Honouring our parents means to hold them in respect and it is for our lifetime. In young children, the way to honour their parents takes the form of obeying them.

2. **How serious was disobedience to parents as an offence in the Old Testament law (Deut. 21:18-21)?** A rebellious son is defined as one who would not listen to the voice of his father

Session 13: Ephesians 6:1-9

or mother even though they discipline him (Deut. 21:18). He faced a death sentence by stoning (Deut. 21: 21) for breaking the fifth commandment. This sounds ghastly to our standard today, doesn't it? What was the reason for the punishment? *So you shall purge the evil from your midst, and all Israel shall hear, and fear* (Deut. 21:21). It is there to warn that a rebellious son embodies evil in him and is a threat to the community. Can we say there isn't wisdom in that? A child who grows up with a sense of respect for and obedience to his parents will have learnt the right attitude towards the authority of other leaders and the rights of other people in general. Today we hear more of children's rights than responsibilities, and the message to children is that they can be whatever they want to be. If the adults heed to that, children are effectively put in charge. The Bible is clear that parents must discipline their children, and we must also pray for their hearts that they will not be rebellious children as defined here. Our role is to guide our children on the path of self-discovery on the person whom God has intended them to be, and that would not move outside of the Bible because God can never contradict Himself. Disobedience to parents is indeed an early sign of disobedience to any authority in general and this trait spells trouble ahead.

Fathers discipline (6:4)

3. **Since children are to obey their 'parents' (6:1), why does Paul address only** *fathers* **in 6:4?** This reflects the background of Paul's day when a father had life and death power over his entire household. He could cast out any member of his household, sell them as slaves, or even kill them, and he was accountable to no one. A newborn was placed at his feet to await the pronouncement of its fate – to be kept or to be discarded. Paul was addressing fathers to use their authority over their household for Christ and full of

grace instead of for self. What Paul teaches here was a totally new concept for his original readers. For today's readers, father is commanded to take the role as the head of the household in Paul's teaching, so this lesson is also relevant to the new order of the family.

4. **Fathers are commanded not to provoke their children to anger. In what ways should fathers restrain themselves?** Power presents a huge temptation, so it must be tempered by orderly order. As Paul has commanded children to obey, there is a danger that the authority is used to lord it over them. Paul warns the fathers not to provoke their children in order that they won't be discouraged (Col. 3:21). That is, in no way should fathers demean or destroy their children. Common ways to provoke the children are many: threats, indifference, neglect, favouritism, unreasonableness, a critical spirit, abuse of any forms, emotional blackmail, emotional manipulation, and so on. In disciplining a child, there may also be danger of rules without grace. Paul warns fathers to be aware of their own sins and always look to God on how to exercise fatherly love.

5. **What does Paul call fathers to do?** *Train up a child in the way he should go; even when he is old he will not depart from it* (Prov. 22:6). As we have seen in this letter, a negative is always followed by a positive to give us the direction where we should turn. Fathers are commanded to *bring them up in the discipline and instruction of the Lord*. The word *discipline* literally means 'child-training', while the word *instruction* 'to place in the mind' with a view to transform behaviour. Whatever children know are taught to them. Childhood is a time for learning. If parents do not rise up to teach their own children, the world certainly will. The discipline and instruction are not ours or of the world but *of the Lord*. This again must be alien to Paul's original readers who were

Session 13: Ephesians 6:1-9

Gentile believers and were not brought up under the Law. Now they had to, as we do too, turn to the model father of the Old Testament, who demonstrated the task to us. He poured out his heart and soul in raising his children. He cared about his children deeply, not only for their temporal but also spiritual wellbeing. By word and example, he imparted to them biblical wisdom to steer through the vicissitudes of life. A relationship with God was at the centre of his worldview and children would be made aware of sin and temptation, and how to deal with it.

In fulfilling the role, we soon realise how demanding it is. It is like a mirror that reflects back on us our own devotion to the disciplines of the Lord in our lives. It will not be flattering but the wellbeing of our children will spur us on to grow fast in the Lord in order that we may be more adequate parents to them! It will drive us to the Word and devour it as quickly and as much as our capacity allows us. This is the picture of orderly love from parents to children as it directs both parents and children to grow in Christ.

6. **Application: Are children spoilt these days? What do we observe as the impact of the spoilt generation on the society? What needs to be restored?** Children of our culture have been children of peacetime and affluence. Ours is also an age that emphasises their rights rather than responsibilities. We can think of being 'spoilt' as a mindset rather than certain behaviour. Put simply, it is a mindset of entitlement, that 'I deserve whatever I want'. It follows that 'spoilt' children centre on self with less empathy and sympathy for others. They are also impulsive and lack self-control. The expectation of instant gratification only amplifies this trait. Children who are incessantly told they can do whatever they wish and can have their own way are children who will soon defy their parents, teachers, moral standards,

the law and society in general. Being eager to befriend children, adults may imitate children, rather than the other way round, losing their impact and influence on children. When the world revolves around children to please them in order to gain their approval and acceptance, they effectively rule the adults with their standard, conduct and reasoning. It leaves us to stare at a situation whereby adults are terrified of children either by their aggression or fragility. Children will grow up to be adults (really quickly!) and may become parents one day. A generation of 'spoilt' children – undisciplined, unprincipled, impulsive and disobedient – will produce a society that is chaotic, even destructive. To reverse that, it starts with home: *Fathers, do not provoke your children to anger, but bring them up in the discipline and instruction of the Lord* (6:4). That is, fathers need to father, mothers need to mother their children, and parents who parent their children are not their friends! We will find that children who respect and obey their parents will go on to build a better, safer and more orderly society than our current disintegrating and divisive one.

Slaves and Masters (6:5-9)

7. **Why is Paul's teaching here controversial in his day and ours? How would you defend Paul?** 'Slaves' is a word that carries a strong negative connotation in our society today. The European and American slave trade that lasted past the middle of the nineteenth century was an acrimonious chapter in our history that its ripple effects on our social relations have not fully passed even after two centuries. Slavery is at least as old as written history, if not even older. Slaves were a fixture in the Roman Empire. Julius Caesar reportedly shipped back to Rome somewhere in the region of a million slaves a century before Paul wrote this letter to the Ephesians. Slave made up anywhere between twenty and thirty-five

percent of the population and gradually became indispensable in the functioning of the entire empire. In this context, it is not hard to imagine that they covered a wide variety of roles which ranged from the unskilled menial labour to the highly skilled professionals. 'Some of them became learned men who served in skilled capacities in education and civil service; some were able to accumulate considerable wealth or influence. Felix, for example, the Roman governor of Judea, before whom Paul appeared (Acts 23:23ff), was once a slave but had managed to establish his freedom and gain political position.'[54] Therefore, on the contrary to our common assumption, many Roman slaves were not economically and socially degraded as in some cultures. But this does not mean that others were not humiliated and harshly, sometimes brutally, treated also. After all, slaves were traded, used and discarded as if tools and commodities. Their fate was at the mercy of their masters.

The point of contention for today is that Paul does not renounce slavery but seems to go even further as to endorse it by his teaching here. Paul's original readers might also be asking if their bondage in slavery was congruous with their newfound freedom and status in Christ. In Paul's defence, he was not concerned about reforms in the social institutions but in the persons; the effect of the former is temporal while that of the latter is eternal. His primary concern was that people came to the saving faith, freeing people not by social reforms but by the gospel, and that people were instructed on their new walk in whatever stations they found themselves in a household. *Only let each person lead the life that the Lord has assigned to him, and to which God has called him ... Each one should remain in the condition in which he was called. Were you a*

---

[54] Ferguson, Sinclair, ibid., p. 167.

slave when called? Do not be concerned about it. (But if you can gain your freedom, avail yourself of the opportunity.) For he who was called in the Lord as a slave is a freedman of the Lord. Likewise he who was free when called is a slave of Christ (1 Cor. 7: 17, 20-22). Slaves were very much a part of the household in his day. Whether one was a slave or master, Paul reminded them they no longer walked like the Gentiles did (4:17). In our time, slavery is outlawed everywhere and few households have live-in 'servants'. But we have bosses in workplace and/or we are bosses to our hired hands. Paul's commands in this section are relevant to our sphere of work.

8. **What are the marks of a Christian slave (or worker) (6:5-7)? How was the teaching revolutionary then and now?** Our relationship with Christ rewrites all our earthly relationships, bringing the transformation. It concerns not so much about new things that we do as to our new attitudes in which we discharge our responsibilities. How we work now reflects on our Lord and not our earthly masters.

- We are to *obey [our] earthly masters with fear and trembling. Fear* can mean anything from loving reverence to real terror. In light of how Paul uses the phrase *fear and trembling* elsewhere (Phil. 2:12 and 2 Cor. 7:15), it refers to Christian disposition to the Lord, 'a loyalty whose nervousness lies in the thought that a loved one might be let down.'[55] Slaves in Paul's day were forced to submit and obey probably by threats, brute force and their lack of legal rights. Theirs was reluctant submission and obedience towards an enemy rather than family. Asking them to obey out of loyalty and reverence would be like alien language to their hearts and minds! Although they might be slaves, the household was susceptible to their disloyalty and scheming. Today, we have more rights, but

---

[55] Ferguson, Sinclair, ibid., p. 169.

it does not rule out unreasonable bosses we may work under.
- This obedience is not an outward gesture but *with a sincere heart, as you would Christ*. God requires truth and sincerity of heart. When we serve our masters faithfully, we obey God even if our earthly masters may be terrible and unreasonable, and do not command our respect!
- Our drive has also changed: *not by the way of eye-service, as people-pleasers, but as servants of Christ* (v6a). We as servants of Christ are not looking to please men but our new and perfect Master. There are no two faces, or cheating and slacking just because we are not found out. Instead, tasks will be completed to the best of our ability independent of whether people are looking or not, that is, our performance is *honest work with [our] own hands* (4:28) from the heart and not deceitful practice: *doing the will of God from the heart, rendering service with a good will as to the Lord and not to man* (v6b-7). This is in contrast to the ill-will a slave may have against his master.

9. **What is the motivation (6:8)?** Whether our good work is seen or rewarded by our earthly masters is immaterial to our work attitude. In that there is a sense of freedom. Paul points the 'slaves' to their eternal hope in heaven and their inheritance. Their incentive is not set for earthly but heavenly rewards, and God will not overlook anything but will always be appropriate. And in God's kingdom, 'no distinction is made between a slave and a free man. The world is wont to set little value on the labours of slaves; but God esteems them as highly as the duties of kings. In His estimate, the outward station is thrown aside, and each is judged according to the uprightness of his heart.'[56] The command is to serve with an integrity fitting for their new identity, i.e. to be worthy of the

---

[56] Calvin's commentary on Ephesians.

calling to which they have been called (4:1). Their spiritual freedom is secure even if they are still slaves to their earthly masters. How exhilarating to look to the promise, *knowing that whatever good anyone does, this he will receive back from the Lord, whether he is slave or free* (v8).

10. **What is the command to the masters of slaves (v9)? Why is this revolutionary to our practice?** 'Though no royal edicts had ever been issued for the protection of slaves, God allows to masters no power over them beyond what is consistent with the law of love.'[57] Christian masters are commanded to *do the same to [the slaves]* they own, treating them as they would have been treated. The reason provided by Paul is that masters and slaves have the same heavenly Master, who see no difference between masters and slaves: *there is no partiality with him*. In other words, they are equal in God's sight. Therefore, *stop your threatening* as the law of love is the only true standard. This is revolutionary for anyone who is in a position of authority to use it not for self but for Christ and for the good of those whom Christ loves. They have the same Master in heaven, to whom they must give an account.

In the spirit of 5:21, Paul always addresses both sides of an earthly relationship: wives and husbands, children and fathers, and slaves and masters. One-sided effort will not make this work. God's impartiality is a fitting truth to close this section on Spirit-filled earthly relationships as all are equally subservient to a common Master, our Lord and Saviour, Jesus Christ, in whatever roles we are serving. We should not be exploitative in any relationships but seek to serve others out of reverence for Christ.

---

[57] Calvin's commentary on Ephesians.

Session 13: Ephesians 6:1-9

Applications

11. Are there new insights into your parent-child relationship from today's study? What will you do differently at home with your children?

12. What kind of boss do you have and what kind of boss are you? In what ways may you improve your work relations?

13. Do you feel like a slave to anything? How can you break free by renewing your mind?

14. Spiritual Warfare [6:10-24]

In the second half of this letter, Paul expounded to the first-century believers what the Christian manner of walk looked like, one *worthy of the calling to which [they] [had] been called* (4:1). Having studied his imperatives, we cannot help but realise how radical this transformation is and Paul is describing none other than a new kingdom order for the followers of Christ Jesus. *The old has passed away; behold, the new has come* (2 Cor. 5:17b). The new order is not marked by incremental or inconspicuous changes, but by a major departure from our former way of life in darkness (e.g. 4:21-24, 5:8)! When we contemplate what it means to live out the new order, we are confronted with the formidable challenge to uproot what is deep-seated inside us and overthrow what is well-established as the social patterns around us. Although light has dawned, everywhere else is still shrouded in deep darkness. By following Paul's teaching up to this point, we should naturally see our situation as besieged by the dark forces more clearly. By exhorting us to live a life worthy of our calling, Paul has opened up our vision to see the spiritual battle between light and darkness that is at hand. We may have been ignorant of it, but now we should see why we are called Christ's church militant on this side of heaven.

If we have read Paul correctly, we will ask the questions he foresees us to ask, the answer to which he readily provides. To conclude the letter, Paul does not leave believers to helplessly fend for themselves in the spiritual battle but arm them to stand firm in the fight. The question for us is whether we are ready to answer the clarion call by joining the ranks to arm and resist the devil.

Self-reflective questions

How real is the spiritual warfare to you? What are your personal battlefronts?

What has been your strategy so far? Do you feel helpless or confident?

The warfare of believers (6:10-13)

1. **'As believers grow stronger, so will Satan's attack.' Discuss (6:12).** While the aim of Christ is to save a people of His own possession from perishing into the eternal abyss, the aim of Satan mirrors Christ's to keep as many in captivity to perish with him. This cosmic conflict between the Lord and the serpent takes place in *the heavenly places* (v12). Its context is set from Genesis 3:15 onwards and by the end of the Scriptures, the serpent has grown into the size of a dragon in Revelation 12:9! While there is no salvation for the fallen angels, Christ has come and accomplished God's salvation plan for the human race. He has already struck the deathblow to the powers of darkness, but they are not yet finally destroyed. While the victory is sure, it has to be played out. Those who have been saved were once children of wrath (2:3), following the prince of the power of the air (2:2, and also S4Q2) but no longer (4:17). They are now in the camp of 'the opposition', consequently facing the rage and attack of Satan. Having suffered the deathblow from Christ, Satan strikes with great wrath because he knows his time is short (Rev. 12:12). Satan hates God, but God cannot be hurt or harmed. Instead, Satan targets God's chosen people whom God loves dearly. Satan's schemes are to make believers ineffective in following and serving Christ, sowing doubts, inflicting costs and frustrating their Christian walk. The battlefronts are nothing mystical or ethereal but in the mundane routine of our daily life as Paul has besought us to guard in Chapters 4 and 5 – in our hearts, in our resolve, in our homelife that make up our daily walk.

Therefore, personal struggles of believers are set in a much bigger context of this cosmic war. As Satan keeps a tight grip on his powers of darkness, he hinders the advancement of the gospel that snatches people out of his hold and puts them into God's kingdom. As believers grow in obedience to Christ and become His effective servants, this foils Satan's scheme and we can only expect Satan to intensify his attack on them. 'As believers grow stronger, so will Satan's attack.' We cannot understand this conflict by what is seen but by what is unseen, and only the Bible gives us the perspective from the heavenly realm. *For we do not wrestle against flesh and blood, but against the rulers, against the authorities, against the cosmic powers over this present darkness, against the spiritual forces of evil in the heavenly places* (v12). The realm where spiritual blessings are received (1:3) is also the location where this ongoing spiritual battle is fought out. That is to say, our greatest enemy is not of the world we see, corrupt and wicked as it is, but of the world we cannot see. <u>We face an uneven contest</u>. Jesus alludes to this cosmic struggle when He promises that 'I will build my church and the gates of hell shall not prevail against it' (Matt. 16:18). No one can be an onlooker; there is no neutral ground to be claimed. Either we belong to Christ or Satan, to the kingdom of light or the kingdom of darkness (5:7-14). His people are at war and will continue to be so until Christ returns.

The Greek word which is translated as *wrestle* was used of hand-to-hand combat, characterised by trickery and deception. In ancient Rome, the conflict was real and a matter of life for the winner and death for the loser.[58] [59] It would not

---

[58] MacArthur, John, ibid., p.340.

[59] 'Plutarch tells us, (Symp. 1.2, page 638) that wrestling was the most artful and subtle of all the ancient games, and that the name of it was derived from a word, which signifies to throw a man down by deceit and craft. And it is certain that persons who understand this exercise have many fetches, and turns, and changes of posture, which they make use of to supplant and trip up their adversaries. And it is with great justice, that a state of persecution is compared with it; since many are the arts, arising from the terrors of worldly evil on the one hand, and the natural love which men have to life, liberty, plenty, and the pleasures of life, on the other, that the devil makes use of to circumvent and foil them.' – Chandler. (Calvin's commentary on Ephesians, footnote 170.)

be profitable to analyse too closely the terms Paul uses here: *rulers, authorities, powers* and *forces*. These terms suggest that Satan is a formidable enemy with his powers well and strategically organised. And as long as he has power, we know it will be *evil day* (v13) with no ends to chaos, confusion, strife, antagonism, division and war.

2. **What is the character of the devil as our enemy (6:11-12)?** Reconnaissance – knowing as much as possible about our enemy – is an important element in any warfare. From these verses, we can surmise the following about the devil:
   - He possesses supernatural power, *for we do not wrestle against flesh and blood* (v12). And yet his powers are as far as God permits.
   - He is a good tactician with well-organised strategy as suggested by the rankings in the terms of *rulers, authorities, powers* and *forces*.
   - He schemes against God and therefore those who love God (v11). His schemes are effective on us because he knows the nature of our flesh so well that we easily fall for them should we not be on guard. Learning from Adam and Eve's experience in Genesis 3, the schemes of the devil can be summed up into five things that they seek to destruct:[60]
      i. The Word of God and its reliability;
      ii. The character of God and His generosity;
      iii. The righteousness of God and His absolute dependability;
      iv. The enjoyment of God and its abundant pleasures;
      v. The fellowship of the people of God and its harmony and unity.
   - It is worth remembering that the battle is not ours but God's (2 Chron. 20:15).

---

[60] Ferguson, Sinclair, ibid., p. 176.

Session 14: Ephesians 6:10-24

3. **Where is our source of strength in this battle (6:10)?** Proud as we are, we often turn to our own strength as the first resort in times of trouble. But if we have truly understood the nature of our struggle, i.e. it is not against flesh and blood (v12), we would know that relying on our own strength is a lost cause. Our tactics is to know that it is God's battle and so it can only be fought in God's power and in His armour. *In the Lord* and *in the strength of his might* (v10) is the only possible way to withstand the onslaught of Satan's attack and schemes. We cannot excuse ourselves on the grounds of inability as Paul asks nothing of ourselves but to *be strong in the Lord*. If our confidence is *in the strength of his might*, we have no reason to shrink from the combat unless the God in our minds is too small and of no match for the devil, which of course is absurd. Let us recall what this *immeasurable greatness of power* is in 1:20-21: *that he worked in Christ when he raised him from the dead and seated him at his right hand in the heavenly places, far above all rule and authority and power and dominion, and above every name that is named, not only in this age but also in the one to come.*

4. **What does Paul call on us to do in this war and what is the provision for it (6:11, 13)?** Paul does not call us to win the battle. Given that it is a cosmic conflict, it is not a battle that we can win ourselves. He only calls us to *stand* (v11) and *to stand firm* (v13). Why is this so? It is because the victory is already won by Christ's works on earth. It is complete; it is finished with nothing else left to do. All that we have to do is to *stand* the ground of the victory Christ has already won. To stand may sound easy but when is standing difficult? Standing is hard when we have to *withstand* (v13) the pressure that is pushed against us as *in the evil day* (v13). The harder we are pressed against, the more strength we need to exert in order to hold down the critical position without giving an inch. Standing is also hard when we are feeble on

our feet due to our internal weakness and we may fall by ourselves. Whichever way, the aim of the devil is to see us knocked down and lose the ground of victory Christ has already won.

Hard as it may be, Paul does not counsel us to give up but to be prepared for battle, energised by the hope of victory already won. Using military metaphors, Paul beseeches us to *put on the whole armour of God* (vv11&13), the only way *that [we] may be able to withstand in the evil day* (v13). We do not put on and put off as we see fit. This is no peacetime, and therefore, the armour of God is our <u>permanent</u> attire. Furthermore, Paul bids us to put on the *whole* armour of God, in order that we leave no glaring weakness open for the devil's attack. If we put our confidence in the Lord throughout our life, i.e. *having done all*, we will find that no danger may not be met successfully by the power of God, and in turn we are able *to stand firm* (v13).

Application: Do we exhibit Christian readiness in this spiritual warfare that Paul speaks of? Are we alert to *the schemes of the devil* (v11), which may attack in open warfare as well as in ambush and stealth? Our enemies are such as no human power can withstand. Unprepared believers surely become defeated believers in confrontation. How do we put on the armour? <u>God's strength is made available to us through our obedience to Him in our daily walk.</u> Are we sluggish in taking up His offered grace?

The armour of God (6:14-17)

5. **Whom does Paul call to take up the armour of God in this passage?** Throughout this letter, Paul frequently addresses his readers in second person 'you'. But more specifically it is second person *plural* ('you all'), i.e. all who are in the church.

Session 14: Ephesians 6:10-24

It does not mean that Paul's teaching lacks the personal dimension to each of us individually; we must take to heart of his exhortations for ourselves. However, we must not lose sight of this new entity created by Christ's redeeming work (2:11-22). Paul calls us to maintain the unity of the church (4:3). This is especially true and important when it comes to spiritual conflict. No army is made up of one person, and any weakness in the army is like a gap in the armour inviting the enemy to attack. This battle we are engaged in as God's people is not a personal battle but a collective one. It is not good enough that our personal walk is in order and we individually are standing firm; how about our local church to which we belong and other churches? As we lift our heads and look around, we will see our collective united front has many cracks which the enemy has breached. In this analysis, we cannot help but lament that we have lost much ground while the enemy has gained much.

6. **What make up the armour of God and what protection does each part offer (6:14-17 cf. Isa. 59:17)?** *He put on righteousness as a breastplate, and a helmet of salvation on his head; he put on garments of vengeance for clothing, and wrapped himself in seal as a cloak.* Isaiah 59:17 describes the clothing of the anointed conqueror, and we can see some striking similarities to the armour of God we are called to put on here. We are clothed like our Commander-in-Chief in this battle. Our armour is not external clothing, but our well-wrought Christian inner qualities publicly revealed. Christ has modelled it for us as He worked in the ranks as a common soldier when He walked on earth. We are His regular army now, trained by Him and bearing His distinction. How are we shaping up in answering this clarion call?

The armour is largely for defence with only one offensive weapon. It would be unwise to fill up the imagery with our imagination but the main lines of what Paul says are clear. The first three pieces of armour are to be put on and never to be taken off on the battlefield, while the last three are to be taken up in actual combat.

- **The belt of truth** – *having fastened the belt of truth* can be translated as 'having girded your loins with truth'. The Roman soldier wore a tunic which posed a potential danger in close combat if left loose. When went to war, it needed to be tucked into the heavy leather belt that girded the soldier's loins. It can be seen as a metaphor of self-discipline and total commitment to the truth, against mediocrity, indifference, lukewarmness and lethargy. 'With your loins girded' also reminds us of Exodus 12:11 and Luke 12:35, both of which convey readiness for action. *Truth* refers to the gospel truth as well as truthfulness in character that produced by it, namely, integrity and consistency. Without this, we individually and collectively as a church are open to Satan's accusation of hypocrisy.

- **The breastplate of righteousness** – The breastplate protects our vital organs from fatal wounds. Is 'righteousness' Christ's or ours? It could be both weaved together as a whole (Rev. 12:11). Satan is 'the accuser of our brothers' who has been conquered by the blood of the Lamb and the word of testimony of the saints (Rev. 12:10). We are justified in Christ's righteousness, which protects us from Satan's malicious accusation to rouse our guilt. We subsequently grow in practical righteousness of a life lived in obedience to God's Word.

- **The shoes of gospel readiness** – In combat, we need shoes of good grip for secure footing, which allow the soldier to be ready for any situation, whether to march, climb or fight. Besides, our target for this war is to *stand firm*. Good

Session 14: Ephesians 6:10-24

shoes fitting for the battle are provided by our firm grip on the *gospel of peace*, in order that we will be 'ready in season and out of season' (2 Tim. 4:2) and 'always prepared to make a defence to anyone who asks you for a reason for the hope that is in you' (1 Pet. 3:15). This gospel is one that brings <u>peace</u>, not violence, for this gospel age, as now is *the year of the* LORD's *favour*, as opposed to *the day of vengeance of our God* (Isa. 61:2).

- **The shield of faith** – Roman soldiers used several kinds of shields, of which two were the most common. The first kind was a small round shield of two feet in diameter secured to the arm by two leather straps. They were used in close body combat. The second kind was door-sized shield of four feet by two and half feet, made of solid wood covered with metal or heavy oiled leather. This was the kind that Paul refers to here. They were used to form a solid wall of defence in a tight-knit phalanx which could extend to a mile long or more. Anyone who stood or crouched behind the wall of shields was protected from *all the flaming darts of the evil one*. Showers of arrows, dipped in pitch and lighted, were commonly fired at the enemies in battle. The wall of shields covered with metal or leather soaked in water was the most effective defence against these flying arrows, either to deflect them or *extinguish* them.

What then are these *flaming darts of the evil one*? They are primarily temptations fired at us by the devil, each of which directly or indirectly is the temptation to doubt and distrust God and His Word. These could be attacks on the mind, thoughts, and affections of a believer, tempting him to sin and to forget who he is in Christ, creating shame and spiritual paralysis. In face of these attacks, the only protection is *the shield of faith*, that the believer resolutely trusts in Lord Jesus and the power of the gospel that all promises are yes in Christ.

These *flaming darts of the evil one* can be aimed at churches as well. For a church to stand firm, it is not enough that individual members are well guarded but *all* are, otherwise there are gaps in the wall of defence put up by the shields of faith. Reading Christ's letters to the seven churches in Revelation 2-3, we identify the common ways for churches to fall away: losing the first love for Christ, aping the world, tolerating sins, living on past reputation, and lukewarm hearts to all things of Christ. Both Jesus and apostles have warned churches of wolves living among them and that false teachers usually come out from them. Enemies are both inside and outside of the church. This makes guarding hard. In our day, we lament the health of the churches in our nation. There are those visibly fallen away from faith on gender issues, for example, but there are also those less visibly sidestepping away from Christ-centrality and truth to make faith about activities, self, social agenda and political correctness. It is also an easy mistake to lose what we seek by the way we seek it.

- **The helmet of salvation** – A helmet is to protect us from head injury which can be so easily fatal. Paul stresses the importance of the mind in our Christian life; we are transformed by the renewal of our minds (4:23). Satan can surely attack our minds and thoughts, telling us many lies and crooked ways that we could believe to be true. In long-standing democratic societies, the majority has much power and is often taken to be 'right'. The pressure to conform can be relentless, both for individuals and for churches. This is when our knowledge and understanding are most tested. Our ability to apply God's Word to our

Session 14: Ephesians 6:10-24

situations is spiritual discernment. The certainty of our salvation is the protection of our heads in an age of ambiguity and absurdity, so that we don't lose our minds but can see straight and clear. To possess the mind of Christ (1 Cor. 2:16) is our best protection.

- **The sword of the Spirit**, which is the word of God – This is the only offensive weapon in the armour of God. The *sword* here is *machaira*, which varied in length from six to eighteen inches. It was the common sword carried by Roman foot soldiers in a sheath or scabbard attached to their belts. Being the principal weapon in hand-to-hand combat, it was always at hand and ready for use.[61]

There are times when the best form of defence is to attack. God's Word is the most effective way to force Satan to retreat. There is power in His Word. Jesus demonstrates it to perfection when He was tempted in the wilderness (Matt. 4:1-11). Shouldn't we learn from our Commander-in-Chief how to stand our ground? It is also the only way to ensure that we are not ignorant of Satan's schemes (2 Cor. 2:11); knowing our enemy is essential for both defence and offence. Verse 17 teaches that through the Word is the way the Spirit works. That is, He brings to our remembrance God's Word and teaches us its meaning and application (John 14:26) from the situations of our life. He never teaches anything that is contradictory to the Scriptures. <u>Effective and fruitful Christians must be well-versed in Scripture, or they are effectively disarmed against Satan's attack</u>. I cannot see there is any other way. but I hear many hesitations that discount this call to know the Scriptures as essential to Christian walk: e.g. 'I am not academic', 'We must not use Bible jargon', 'The Gospel

---

[61] MacArthur, John, ibid., p. 367-368.

must be made relevant and accessible for our day', 'We must not discount simple faith', 'Scripture is difficult to understand', 'Bible handling is reserved for the professionally trained', 'Theology is cold', 'Doctrines divide', 'I have no time', and the list goes on. For whatever reasons that make us hesitate, remember that God asks us to *be strong* not in ourselves but *in the Lord and in the strength of His might* (6:10).

God reveals Himself in two ways: in His creation and in His Word. The former is enough to condemn us but not enough to save us. God could have chosen other forms but He has chosen to speak to us in His Word. If we do not know His Word, we cannot know Him. 'There is no man of any rank who is not bound to be a soldier of Christ. But if we enter the field unarmed, if we want our sword, how shall we sustain that character?'[62] Therefore, any 'reasoning' that convinces us to keep our bible closed is doing Satan's bidding. There is a lot of wisdom in J. C. Ryle's observation that 'A Bible-reading laity is the strength of a church.'[63] In spiritual warfare, let all, not just the leaders, be armed with *the sword of the Spirt, which is the word of God,* [64] because all of us are Christ's soldiers and weak links expose the army to attack.

---

[62] Calvin's commentary on Ephesians, available online.

[63] J. C. Ryle *Warnings to the Churches*, The Banner of Truth Trust (2016), p.77.

[64] '... it is not without reason that the most necessary instruments of warfare – a sword and a shield – are compared to faith, and to the word of God. In the spiritual combat, these two hold the highest rank. By faith we repel all the attacks of the devil, and by the word of God the enemy himself is slain. If the word of God shall have its efficacy upon us through faith, we shall be more than sufficiently armed both for opposing the enemy and for putting him to flight' (Calvin's commentary on Ephesians, available online).

Prayer in warfare (6:18-20)

Paul begins the letter by lifting our eyes up to see the lofty things in the heavenlies, and he ends by pulling us down to our knees in earnest prayer.

7. **What is the role of prayer in spiritual warfare (6:18)? What and how should we pray?** Prayer is not seen as part of the armour of God, but it is what brings the whole armour to life and work as it should be. 'Our divine gifts – marvellous as they are – are bare without the divine Giver.'[65] Verse 18 perhaps is the most comprehensive single sentence on how we are to pray! There are four 'alls' in this verse for emphasis:
- We are to pray *at all times*. Prayer is a lifestyle and not merely an action to call upon on occasions. It is an overflow of how we live our whole life in the presence of God, constantly setting our minds on things above and not things on earth (Col. 3:2). Prayer is a dialogue with God which interacts tightly with His Word. Prayer is a means of grace that brings us into communion with God. Our private prayer life lays the foundation of our public corporate prayer life.
- We are to pray *in the Spirit*. The function of our prayer is not for our will but God's will to be done! How do we know God's will? We can't: *For my thoughts are not your thoughts, neither are your ways my ways, declares the LORD. For as the heavens are higher than the earth, so are my ways higher than your ways and my thoughts than your thoughts* (Isa. 55:9). So, we often don't know how to pray. But we are not without help: *For who knows a person's thoughts except the spirit of that person, which is in him? So also no one comprehends the thoughts of God except the Spirit of God* (1 Cor. 2:11). To pray, we need the Spirit's help in our

---
[65] MacArthur, John, ibid., p. 378.

weakness (cf. Rom. 8:26-27), being Spirit-filled (5:18), relying on His power and wisdom and not our own.
- We are to pray *with all prayer and supplication*. This means to offer prayers of all kinds. One acronym to capture the breadth of prayer is ACTS – Adoration, Confession, Thanksgiving and Supplication. Such prayer is a balanced reflection of God's character and our relationship with Him. Prayer of this order is a full and disciplined life of communion with God.
- Our prayer life is sustained by us *keep[ing] alert with all perseverance*. In preparing for His departure, Jesus urged His disciples to 'Be on your guard, keep awake' (Mark 13:33) and 'Watch and pray that you may not enter into temptation' (Mark 14:38). Alertness is always essential when living in a war zone; Christ is building His church in territory occupied by His archenemy! There will be trials and hardship, pressing us to give up. Against this, we need to press on *with all perseverance*. It implies a resolute determination to see something through to its bitter end. Even though our victory is sure, our perseverance will be a proof of that.
- We are to *[make] supplication for all the saints*. Paul twice sets an example of this in this letter (1:15-23 and 3:14-21). Once again, Paul stresses that we are not in spiritual warfare as lone fighters but together as a unit. We are a united front fighting together under the command of Christ. <u>All</u> the saints are engaged in this warfare; we are comrades, even if in different locations. It broadens our sphere of concerns beyond our earthly needs to align with Christ's concerns. It lifts our eyes to things above and engage our attention on the advancement of God's kingdom. Given that prayer is love, this encourages the communion of saints and seals it with our love for them.

8. **What does Paul teach us by asking his readers to pray for him (6:19-20)?** It is natural for believers to think of Paul as the 'mighty apostle' and view him in awe. But Paul is not afraid of exposing his weaknesses and vulnerabilities. We are to pray for *all saints* and that includes himself. He was weak; he had been distressed and despaired. At times, he was lonely and afraid. He needed prayer from his fellow saints as much as others to strengthen him. But he did not ask for improvement of his situation or supply to his physical needs. In the context of spiritual warfare, he asks fellow believers to pray for his ministry. He asks for prayer on two specific things: *words* and *boldness*.

He does not ask for *words* just as something to say but penetrating, clear and faithful words that bring *the mystery of the gospel* to light in people's minds with the Spirit's power to convict and transform. From a personal situation of being *in chain*, he asks for *boldness* that he may not be deterred by the potential hostile reception of the hearers and consequences to himself and remove the offence of the cross (Gal. 5:11). He has not forgotten that he is *an ambassador* of Christ; though *in chain*, he desires to remain blameless in discharging his duty by asking for *boldness* to speak what he *ought to speak*. We have learnt from the study of this letter how revolutionary and radical his message is to the people then and now.

Final greetings (6:21-24)

9. **How did Paul keep up his communication with the churches (6:21-22)?** For communication, Paul wrote letters to the churches and his friends. But to him a letter was never a perfect substitute for meeting face to face (see, for example, 1 Thess. 2:17-19). Since he was in chain, he sent his trusted co-worker Tychicus, not only to bring his letters but also his personal news to his friends, many of whom he had not seen

for some time. They were most likely over-anxious for him on the news of his imprisonment. *So that you also may know how I am and what I am doing,* he sent to them Tychicus who had seen and spent time with him to *encourage your hearts;* he would *tell you everything.* Paul supported his prayer for *all* the saints with action to encourage them, and nothing works better than a personal visit. *Everything* about what? All the personal news of Paul, of course, but it could also imply that if there were any questions about the content of the letter, Tychicus *will tell you everything.*

10. **Who was Tychicus and what do we learn about ministry (6:21)?** In the final greetings, we catch a glimpse that ministry is teamwork. Paul had some trusted co-workers in his team and Tychicus was one of them. For the task of delivering the letters and his news, he sent Tychicus whom he called his *beloved brother and faithful minister.* Furthermore, hidden in this seemingly passing reference of no real significance is a proof of Paul living out the gospel of peace and unity he preaches: Tychicus was a gentile and he was a well-trusted member of Paul's gospel team. What is the key gospel message in this letter? Christ has broken down in His flesh the dividing wall of hostility (2:14), so that *the Gentiles are fellow heirs, members of the same body, and partakers of the promise in Christ Jesus through the gospel* (Eph. 3:6). Originally from Asia, Tychicus joined Paul's team of trusted colleagues when he left Ephesus after his lengthy ministry there (Acts 20:4-6). Paul sent him to deliver not only this letter to Ephesus but also the one to Colossae (Col. 4:7-9). Travelling with him was Onesimus, a new convert who was a runaway slave of Philemon. So, apart from carrying Paul's precious teaching to the churches, Tychicus was also entrusted with the task of bringing Onesimus back to Colossae and 'brokering' a deal to return the slave to his Christian master (see the Letter to Philemon). This says a great deal of his Christian character

Session 14: Ephesians 6:10-24

and wisdom on the one hand, and the respect and trust he commanded of Paul and others on the other hand. Paul also frequently sent him on missions (see 2 Tim. 4:12; Titus 3:12). One thing to learn about Paul in ministry is that he was ready to send out his best men to encourage others in advancing the gospel rather than keeping them to himself even in times of needs.

11. **What is in the benediction (6:23-24)?** The letter begins with a doxology – a word of praise to the glory of God. It ends with a benediction – a pronouncement of blessing from God to us. The foundation of *peace* is our reconciliation with God brought to us through *love from God the Father and the Lord Jesus Christ*, which we experience *with faith*. Without *grace*, we would not have been in Christ and brought into the fellowship of His church. When such love is received, it is answered *with love incorruptible* – a genuine love that has been purified and never dies but will last for all eternity.

Applications

12. Are you under Satan's attack in any way? Have you put on the full armour of God? What insight has this study brought into your spiritual battles?

13. According to your assessment, how well is your church prepared for spiritual warfare?

14. What changes has Paul's teaching resulted in your prayer life?

15. In what ways has the whole study on Ephesians impacted you and your Christian walk?